The author now lives essentially on his own, and the previous hobby of antiques has been replaced by philately. He continues with an interest in chess and horticulture and is currently breeding a new strain of Himalayan poppy.

For Dianne Webb, the honest politician.

Richard Lacey

GERM WARS

AUSTIN MACAULEY PUBLISHERS™

LONDON • CAMBRIDGE • NEW YORK • SHARJAH

A CIP catalogue record for this title is available from the British Library.

ISBN 9781528917179 (Paperback)
ISBN 9781528917186 (E-Book)

www.austinmacauley.com

First Published (2019)
Austin Macauley Publishers Ltd
25 Canada Square
Canary Wharf
London
E14 5LQ

I would like to thank a number of people whom I did not know. On two occasions, I was rescued from serious road accidents that were my fault. The second was by the Lancashire police (Chapter 8) and it is not difficult for a person who is not quite a Yorkshire man to say a big thank you. Some colleagues working on issues including listeria, BSE and antibiotics were aware that their involvement could provoke some hostility from big business. It did. I thank them for their persistence. I do not think it damaged their careers.

Finally, I would like to thank Karen Lunn for research and for converting doctor's scribble into type.

Introduction

Why now? True, I have been mentally considering the idea of an autobiography for some years, but it has been the events of the last year or so that have persuaded me to put pen to paper. The expected protracted crisis in the NHS has been an important influence, and I think some of my experience will be relevant to understanding the origins of the problem. It is a rare pleasure for me to applaud government pledges to ensure free expression of opinion at university. However, the interface between university and NHS will always be tricky without trust and good will from both.

The facts and opinions are mine exclusively. There are no ghosts in the machine, and no major organisation has asked me to write this – perhaps there are those who might have wished for silence; I don't think the James Bond film industry will be too impressed by the proposals towards the end of chapter 3. Nor will defenders of the historic boarding school system, nor NHS management.

Apart from responding to a few recent events, the narrative ceases in 1998 on my second retirement. I have always been aware of the problems for scientists well known to the public (I did about 400 TV interviews) when asked about material that they are not familiar with. So this is emphatically not about the so called food 'scares', it is about the experience over a thirty-year career. I have in the main refrained from commenting on recent figures of any sort because I cannot know if those numbers are accurate.

The bulk of the text is factual, although sometimes with parenthetic questions to the 'authorities'. The end of chapter 3 does contain some ideas, as does the final chapter headed CODA. This is a term from classical music whereby after the composer has followed a traditional structure, allows himself a flexible diversion at the end of a piece.

I have had no criticism against any university administration, and I would like to highlight the generosity of Cambridge, and the kindness of Sao Paolo, Brazil. Any problems encountered have been with individuals, usually because of the then dependence on external funding and promotion of their products or even ethic.

R. W. Lacey, Jan 2018

Chapter 1
Early Memories

A shriek, then a terrifying bang, and I was hurled backwards into the house. Then the nasty smell and I was spluttering from the dust. My arm was bleeding – but I was alive. It was 1941 with a major bombing attack around London in World War Two.

At the time, I was a small baby in the pram at the open front door of our house called, 'The Moorings' in Erith, Kent (now Greater London), and, of course, I was recalling events described later to me by my parents. My father was also injured slightly by the blast of the Nazi bomb that had fallen in the corner of the front garden.

I think it is difficult to be certain that early childhood memories are truly yours or are descriptive events – perhaps changed by others. I have always questioned some of the reliability of psychoanalysis based on early childhood memories.

To return to 1941, my father was a general practitioner in Erith, having had a similar post as a Junior GP in Burley Inn Wharfedale from 1936 when he had qualified from Selwyn College, Cambridge and The London Hospital (in Whitechapel). My mother had been a middle ranked nurse, also at The London Hospital. She would at this time have been pregnant with my younger brother, Ian. As a result of the bomb, the family was 'evacuated' to Peebles in the Scottish Borders. Soon, my father was drafted to a British garrison in Poona (now Pune) in Western India, not far from Bombay (now Mumbai). I gather, the military strategy at the time was to develop a medical facility for possible injuries to British soldiers fighting the expected Japanese westward invasion through Northern Thailand, and the British colonies of Burma and the Indian subcontinent. Britain already had a substantial military presence in Burma as reflected in stamps from my collection with the figurehead of George VI and overprinted MILY ADMIN.

My father would become the single most important influence on me, usually, but not always for the good. I think my mother had always fancied being a 'Medical Consultant's' wife; she was always pleased to claim that her husband had 'specialised'! That the Japanese army never conquered the subcontinent, becoming obstructed in Thailand and Burma (the film 'Bridge on the River Kwei' is a good illustration), gave my father the opportunity to research into the newly developed science of blood transfusion. He later received his Cambridge doctorship for this.

My memories of life in Peebles begin, I think, in 1943 with a picture of the plain wooden chair in the kitchen and my mother telling me I was two years old. I wonder what Sigmund Freud would have made of this? I can also visualise containers of food being suspended by string over garden walls, as everyone tried to make the most of wartime rationing. I have vague recollections of neighbours, but nothing specific. However, during the cold winter of 1944, I can remember scraping with my fingers frozen condensation off the inside of windows. In 1945, at the permanent return of my father, memories became more emphatic. The marching of khaki-clad soldiers in the streets of Peebles occurred at about this time, but the actual return of my father was 'celebrated' with fireworks in the garden under fruit trees. I found the bangs terrifying! And I know what followers of Sigmund Freud are thinking – I had been conditioned to hate loud noise by the bomb in Erith in 1941. No, we had a quiet peaceful life up to 1945, and inevitably the sudden experience of alien bangs to a sensitive four year old was obviously offensive.

One incident that troubled me involved my younger brother then aged three. He had a sore throat, and my father being a doctor (and mother a nurse) decided to paint (literally) Ian's throat with some proprietary fluid. Having spent nearly four years in a sunny climate, my father was deeply tanned, and I have complete confidence in recalling some of the words of my brother: "Get that black man out of the house." There is ample evidence from the animal kingdom that unusual or different members of a species can be treated with hostility. So it is with 'Homo sapiens' where prejudice, whether racial, colour, disability or religion is the failure to recognise the existence of instinctive feelings and the failure to control them, hopefully through education.

One principle of behaviour I learnt through my mother was the need to consider how other people feel towards your actions.

Goodbye Peebles.

In late 1945, the Lacey family returned to 'The Moorings', Erith. The Lacey family comprised my father, Jack Westgarth Lacey, my mother, Sybil Lacey (nee Hockey), me, Richard Westgarth Lacey, my younger brother, Ian Westgarth Lacey, and my cat, a non-pedigree black cat my mother had called Peter. Seen from Peter's viewpoint, he considered me his human being.

The purpose of this return to Erith was for my father to tie up loose ends of his general practice and seek formal training in pathology. I have three memories of this interval – first the exact spot from which the bomb had blown me back in to the house, secondly rolling down a slope on the back garden lawn, and thirdly a Victorian conservatory with a defunct water fountain.

In 1946, my father achieved a training post in pathology at The London Hospital, Whitechapel and we moved to a rented semi-detached house in Hampstead. I have no precise memory of schooling that I assume was relatively inexpensive, private and day.

My father's older sister, Marjorie, lived nearby, and all I knew about her then was that she worked for the foreign office. One day I was out with her spaniel dog, called 'Smokey' because of his colour. Another dog attacked Smokey, but I managed to rescue him. Since that incident, I was always close to Aunt Marjorie who never had children.

The winter of 1947 had a substantial impact on me. The prolonged dismal cold and the regular snowfalls gave me an interest in meteorology that has stayed with me till today. After playing in the back garden, almost daily, the tracks on the grass would be recovered with fresh snow. One night in March 1947, with weather warming a little, I awoke being sprayed with water from a burst pipe. Strangely, both in Hampstead and in Peebles, I had no memory of feeling cold despite the evident absence of central heating. Rather, I felt the exhilaration of falling snow.

In media reports in later years of the 1947 winter, school children were taking lumps of coal daily to stoke their school fires. I did not.

In 1948, my father's training was going well and he had plans (promises) or expectation of a consultant post in Chelmsford, to where we moved to a house in Great Baddow, about three miles from the centre of Chelmsford in Essex. I went with my brother to a day school called Saint Ceds in Chelmsford. Our house was called 'Friars Hall' and was on the main road to Maldon. At the front was a low brick wall with pillars and drooping iron chains; at the back of the detached house was a walled piece of ground that was – to be blunt – a building site. My parents must have owned 'Friars Hall', that along with other properties would have been very cheap in this post war period. I still am deeply impressed by the amount of effort my father put into the restoration of the house.

In the evenings, I would see my father wearing his khaki military uniform, now being used for good effect. Gradually over the weeks, the uniform became more and more sprinkled with distemper as were the wooden steps. The conversion of the back 'yard' from building site to garden was near miraculous, and I was becoming very interested in the cultivation of plants. The inside of the boundary walls were planted with loganberries, climbing plants with fruits like a large, dark raspberry.

One afternoon, on returning from school, we found my father's younger brother, Brian, helping himself to loganberries. Brian who had been a doctor based mainly in Egypt during the war, was now doing research at the Westminster Hospital into whooping cough, where he would later become Professor of Microbiology.

Sometimes we went to school by bus that I enjoyed. The bus conductor would announce the names of each stop. We always stopped at the Beehive an Art Deco style public house at a road junction. I was, years later, to become a bus conductor as a student holiday job in Clacton-on-Sea.

We (my brother and I) were, one afternoon, with my mother and we heard gun shots near the bus station. People were running in all directions. Fear gripped us, and I had memories of the fireworks in Peebles. I don't like guns.

I am not sure exactly when this happened. Ian, my mother and I were on a bus together. It could have been Peebles or Erith or Chelmsford. The bus had pulled up at a stop and the engine noise was quiet. Then, suddenly, my brother piped up in a load shrill voice, "Mummy, can we move, the man in front of me smells." Everyone on the bus looked round, and I've never felt so embarrassed in my whole life.

I assume I was happy overall at the school. The only upsetting incident was prior to a Christmas show in 1948; I was dressed up as a type of angel in a tight fitting one-piece outfit with wings! Inevitably if a child is dressed in such a way as to make having a pee difficult, he wants to. I did. The incident happened.

A more amusing incident happened. After changing back from my plimsolls used for running into walking shoes, I put the wrong pair on. This was spotted when I returned home. The hilarity was caused not because they were the wrong shoes, but they were a girl's! I can still remember her name, Patricia Reed, who had worn mine to her home. The exchange back occurred next day.

My father began taking us to school on his way to the Chelmsford and Essex Hospital, often with a small detour to Little Baddow to pick up one of the teachers, Miss Howard. She was the first female I fancied, as did, I think, my father.

Around this time, rationing was getting less and the food industry was recovering its potential. A fizzy drinks' company had its headquarters in Chelmsford and I think the brand name was Corona. Although other children raved about the drink, I never had the chance to try it, not being endorsed by mother who was both conservative and a Conservative. She believed Labour only won the 1945 general election because many voters thought that Winston Churchill would still be prime minister with a labour government. However, both my parents must have benefitted from the NHS, as indeed did the next generation including me.

My father was never politically polarised as much as my mother, tending to vote against the then government – or so he said.

By 1949, we knew that we were to soon move as my father's career was going well. He would have been appalled to see the publicity and recent crisis in 2018 in the NHS. I can see three obvious reasons for this. One is its evident success with the increasingly aged population with greater risk of further illness. Two is the enormous advances in medical techniques, for example, improvement in anaesthetics can enable more patients to be treated. This does not save money because there is a potential limitless need for treatment. Thirdly, the rising U.K. population from immigration, a net figure of around 300,000 per year, and the indigenous birth rate is not sustainable for all infrastructure elements in the long term. I will suggest some ideas to begin to address the problems in the last chapter.

During 1948, my parents began taking me and my brother to see my mother's parents who lived about 40 miles north of Chelmsford in deepest rural Suffolk. The cottage was at the end of a long cul-de-sac called East Green and a few miles from Great Bradley, not far from Haverhill and Newmarket. The cottage was named 'Bramble cottage' and the traditional front aroused memories of paintings by Helen Allingham. But the house told a different story; it seemed to have been assembled from bits of demolished barns with a corrugated iron roof. It was from the roof that all the water was collected. The heating was a range in the main living room. The lighting was a single oil lamp backed up by candles. The toilets were buckets in two garden sheds. The toilet paper was a heap of pieces of newspapers and magazines. The radio was battery operated. However, the garden and grounds were extensive with flower gardens, a vegetable area and fruit trees under which chickens scratched a living. I never did find out the fate of the contents of the toilet buckets!

My grandmother, Laura had been 'in service' that I now interpret to mean a residential servant, a common occupation in the early twentieth century. My grandfather, Tom is said to have designed golf courses, but I suspect some misfortune might have struck prior to their retirement. Both were now in their early seventies. Certainly, they would have been very proud of one of their daughters to succeed in nursing at 'The London Hospital'. Their other five children don't seem to have achieved anything notable.

When my brother and I stayed for anything up to a week, we found the cramped single bed difficult, and I, in particular found the toilet facilities inhibiting! However, exploring the deserted and wild countryside was exciting and we went gleaning – that is scavenging ears of corn missed during the harvest. Exactly how these were converted to usable food remains a mystery, unless the chickens could cope with their crop mechanics!

My grandfather had a very long shed under the fruit trees and we played with toys, garden tools or anything else that came to hand for hours. I can recall a train engine fabricated out of a door bolt!

My grandmother cooked well on the range. Milk came in a churn from the farm opposite and once a week a man from the nearest grocer bought in the groceries. He was named Pawsey and wore a brown-beige coat to look respectable. He would then take next week's order. This system was not unlike internet purchasing today.

Once a week, my grandfather would cycle into Newmarket, where I suspect (now) he had a drink and a gamble. Then one day disaster struck – he was knocked off his bicycle and had very disfiguring bruises that alarmed us all when my parents visited. The good news was that no bones were broken. I think the last time I saw my grandfather was in 1950 when I remember him sitting with his ear on the radio's loudspeaker listening to news of the Korean War.

This experience certainly had an effect on me, in a similar but less significant way to Laurie Lee's Slad in 'Cider with Rosie'.

In 1949, the family began to go on holiday together, initially to Devon, later abroad. My mother would make bacon and egg quiche that my parents enjoyed with a thermos flask cup of tea during the first stop in what seemed an interminable car journey. We always set off very early to 'beat' the traffic – even as early as 4am. It never worked. We would end up in one of the series of 'convoys' of cars on the A30 or A303. The first year our destination was Whitesands on the south Devon coast. The rock pools and marine life fascinated me and building sand buttresses to thwart the incoming tide was exciting. I learnt the art of positioning the excavation at just the right location to stay on the beach as long as possible before watching the inevitable destruction of the 'battlement'.

The beach was amazingly deserted in view of the density of the motor car columns going west. One day, my mother decided to bathe topless, and for reasons I did not understand I found disturbing. Certainly, this was a new experience for me, but the expression on my face must have prevented any recurrence. I still don't know how I felt. In later years, we went to the North Devon coast at Woolacombe, where the volume of sand was greater, but the rock pools and marine life less in evidence. Also the number of holiday makers was on the increase, with a scramble for the optimum base in the sand dunes.

One incident delighted me. It must have been 1952 and as I had been playing table tennis at school I could play in the hotel's games room. On one occasion I was challenged by a Member of Parliament, named I think Richard Shepherd. He lost.

About this time, although my main reading material had been Enid Blyton's Famous Five, I was finding girls of my age or a little bit older, attractive. I remember liking the looks of one girl called Janette. I didn't know what to do about it, so I did nothing. There were too many grown-ups around anyway. What would Laurie Lee have done?

I really looked forward to returning to Great Baddow to see my faithful cat, Peter, now with a few white hairs under his chin. I never knew, or asked, who looked after him (i.e. fed) when the family was away. There are some issues children do accept unquestionably. So was an observation that I made during my whole childhood. That is, neither me nor my brother never had boys or girls visit or stay in our house. Certainly I stayed with other student's families when I was older. The issue was never considered, and in some ways my parents approach to family and friendship was rooted into the 1920s and 1930s. It would take me many years to attempt to compensate for this. However, I frequently visited near neighbours in Great Baddow. Over the road were a retired architect and his wife. I can remember him telling me that his initials were E.P.A and other boys at his school failed to spot the initials when backwards. I sometimes 'helped' him do large adult jigsaws. Another neighbour had a tiny cottage filled with a massive fish aquarium, something I always wanted, but never received.

I maintained my interest in the weather, even listening to the fishing forecast on the BBC home service.

I learnt two facts about the area after leaving Great Baddow. There were the presence of Marconi in Chelmsford and a secret war bunker for our leaders on the outskirts of the village with much electronic and radio capacity.

Chapter 2
Boarding School

In September 1949, my brother and I began boarding at Gadebridge Park, preparatory school near the village of Hemel Hempstead, Hertfordshire about 40 miles west of Chelmsford. I was known as Lacey ma, and Ian as Lacey mi, short for the Latin major and minor. We were the only brothers among around 70 boys. One of these was Crown Prince Sonukul of Siam (now Thailand) who seemed to thrive on his special diet of dried mango. The nephew of the composer of very English classical music, Ralph Vaughan Williams was two years ahead of me.

The school was presumably a conversion from a minor stately home with the addition of a large new wing holding two classrooms downstairs and two dormitories above. The school was approached by a curving drive through parkland dotted with mature trees. Two of these would become goal posts during football 'kick-abouts'.

To the back of the school, there were lawns, trees and shrubs up the slope that led to two sports fields – one for winter football, the other for cricket.

The only communal area was the large dining room where large tables were arranged in a horseshoe shape with new boys at the feet and seniors (aged 12–13) at the top underneath the school honours board. It did not occur to me then that one day, four and a half years later; my name would be above there.

After a few initial difficulties over the dormitory and toilet facilities, I was overall happy. We (Ian and I) would see our parents for an hour or so each half term. We would usually have tea in a cafe. There was one religious service each week. We would adorn straw boaters and troop off to church (except Prince Sonukul) to the village watched with incredulity by local 'real' people. On Sunday afternoon, we wrote letters home. I can remember teasing my parents that I had been using my toothbrush to clean and polish my football boots. Each boy had his own personal 'tuck box', although anything consumable would not last long. Except for one activity, the sports were essentially recreational not disciplinarian, mainly because I think most of the masters were not that interested. However, one young maths master was keen on cricket, and imagine the excitement when several of us found his name in the cricketing almanac Wisden. He was P. A. F Newton.

The best I could do in cricket was to captain the second eleven and score 19. Unfortunately, most of the matches of 1952 were cancelled because of the overzealous quarantine rules over diseases such as German measles.

I did well with lessons and gained several prizes. I still have a special prize for Latin. I was told that I was better at Latin than at English. However, unlike my next school, I was not categorised as a disloyal swot. Incidentally, my affinity for Latin should have come as no surprise, were I to have known about the family ancestry of Lacey. The Laceys came with William the Conqueror to England in 1066 from the LACIUS settlement in Normandy and were known initially as De Lacey. Prior to Normandy we were Roman and the Italian football team 'Lazio' has similar roots, as does the word 'Lascivious' that used to mean sporty! But I digress. What was the activity that troubled me?

Boxing! I can't call it a sport and simply cannot see how some doctors condone it. We were all forced to box; I even had to fight my brother. A barn over a small country lane was the venue and the fights were watched by strangers. I did badly. Then one year, 1951, I think I was to fight a boy known as the school bully. Somehow, I became really angry and the current phrase 'lost the plot' comes to mind. I can't recall the outcome and forgot about it until prize giving. Incredibly I was given a large silver cup for the most improved boxer. My parents kept this for a year. I was acutely embarrassed and confused when relatives and neighbours turned up with acting 'fisticuffs'.

I have little memory of the food at Gadebridge Park. It must have been adequate despite parts of rationing still being enforced. But I do remember the end of sweet rationing. One of the joint headmasters, Humphrey Lindsey weighed out portions of boiled sweets into paper bags. They did not last long.

One area that the school was positive was that of hobbies. I learnt to play chess, table tennis and billiards and the rudiments of book binding. Once or twice a term invited speakers would give us a slide show or even a film. The material often referred to events of World War 2. One military gentleman gave us an entertaining illustrated talk titled 'Gibraltar, Malta and the Island of Cyprus'. My collection of British Empire stamps reflects the importance to national security from the military presence in that area.

In similar vein, one of the masters – indeed our most popular, Major Davenport gave colourful talks on military manoeuvres within his English lesson brief. No doubt they were based on actual events.

In 1953, I took the written examination for a scholarship to Felsted School. I can recall one of the questions; 'Describe in words only the working of a bicycle'. Not so easy! I was later summoned to the oral examination. I had to read out loud to a group of miserable middle-aged masters, a leading article in the Times. I developed a severe stammer. However, I was awarded a small scholarship and saw my name stencilled on the school (Gadebridge Park) honours board. The stammer would take me some time to overcome.

The end of term in March 1954 was beset by a series of heavy snowfalls and after delays; I was overall saddened to leave for the last time. Ian stayed for another year. After five weeks holidays at home, I was in for a nasty shock.

Around 1990, I had been invited to give a talk at the Hemel Hempstead hospital; I could not resist the temptation to look at my old school. It wasn't there, being replaced by a newish housing estate, according to Wikipedia.

'The school had been established by Augustus Orlebar, a former housemaster at Radley College, as a boarding school for boys in Bedford in 1892; it moved to Hinwick House near Wellingborough shortly thereafter and then to Gadebridge House in nearby Hemel Hempstead in 1914. It remained there until it was forced out of its old premises by the Commission for New Towns as part of its development of the new town in 1963. It took on its present name at its present site last year. It is now an independent Prep school which educates boys and girls from rising 3-13 years. The school is in a rural location on 26 acres of parkland overlooking the Bourne valley, off the A41 between Berkhamsted and Hemel Hempstead in Hertfordshire.'

In April 1950, the Lacey family, moved to North Essex, in what could have thought to be an idyllic rural location. The house was about half a mile to the west of the small village of Little Bardfield. During our drive from Chelmsford, we were excited, my eight year old brother Ian referring to our new home as 'Little barleycorn'! We would be about mid-way between Great Bardfield and Thaxted, both around two and a half miles away.

The detached house was set back from the quiet country lane and was constructed of lathe and plaster with walls decorated with pargeted plastering. The roof was thatch and the chocolate-box looking cottage appearance had been built in the 1930s, although it looked older. There were three and a half acres of grounds comprising an incomplete formal garden, and two fields, surrounded by mature trees. There was main water and coal-based central heating. Electricity at 100 volts was purchased from Little Bardfield Hall in the village. Sanitary drainage went into a small septic tank in the front garden that would soon be found inadequate.

There were two other houses nearby, both occupied by retired families. There were no local children. In Little Bardfield Village, there was a church and a small primary school, a pub, a small shop, alms and council houses. Two of these were occupied by a family with 18 children that my mother was amused to say their surname was 'Leek'.

Great Bardfield was becoming famous for its artists. George Chapman painted rather gloomy pictures of streets of mining communities in South Wales. Edward Bawden was a well-known illustrator and John Aldridge, who was self-taught, painted delightfully vivid and precise scenes of local farms and landscapes. Between the Bardfields, the actor Bernard Miles lived in a small house at the end of a long drive up a hill. A retired naval commander called Woolnough lived in a house called 'Chequers' with spectacular topiary.

Thaxted was a delightful small town dating back many centuries, with a large recent council house estate. Delivering letters around here prior to Christmas would become a holiday job for me years later. Although, I only realised this in later years, the English composer Gustav Holst had lived in Thaxted.

Over the years, I met many of the residents of Little and Great Bardfield. There was a predominance of single women, some very elderly, presumably a reflection of the loss of male combatants in both world wars. My parents did not encourage me to meet other children in the village during school holidays, and I can recall only one instance when a boy visited our garden. I met no girls.

The early 1950s saw my father amazingly active at home. He, with a local builder, constructed a new septic tank and drainage system; with help from a gardener from Great Bardfield called Jones, new lawns and flower borders were completed. One of the small fields was converted to a large chicken run for about 100 egg layers, and for a time, a dozen geese.

Main electricity was soon connected; a large wooden greenhouse was located at the end of the vegetable garden now enriched with decomposing chicken manure. In the mid-1950s my father began exhibiting at the annual Great Bardfield horticultural show. I can remember one headline in the local paper 'Green fingered Pathologist wins tops in show'.

At Christmas, my uncle Brian and his social worker 'partner' would bring puzzles and exercises for us all. One year 'we' constructed a three-dimensional model of a virus, and another, a radio!

Aunt Marjorie also came, usually on her own, but gave very generously, particularly to me. In one year I was embarrassed to receive a version of an electric circuit construction toy that was larger than my parent's gift.

I was also interested in gardening, and began collecting cacti usually from cuttings. These were to upset my father because of skin pricking and irritation. My mother looked after my plants during school holidays. These I kept in an old greenhouse down some rickety steps that sometimes I found difficult to negotiate. I was also not enthusiastic about heights when walking along the ruins of Corfe Castle on holiday.

Learning to ride a bicycle caused me considerable problems when aged 10–11. I remember my father spending hours holding the bicycle and running after me.

I did finally manage to cycle, but my balance was such that I always needed a step on a kerb to start. Once riding, the local and near deserted lanes amongst unspoilt countryside and chocolate-box cottages were superb.

Then my near perfect idyll was shattered. At the end of April 1954, I went to Felsted School, an 'all boys' fee paying boarding school about 10 miles away. These still seem to be called 'Public' schools. *Why?* I had thought that with a scholarship, I might be offered some respect. Exactly the opposite happened.

The first shock came with the sleeping arrangements. In our dormitory, in a bed slightly apart from us thirteen year olds, was an older boy, perhaps 17 or 18, a prefect. In the morning he got out of bed and dressed. Then he told us to get out of bed and take our pyjamas off. We then queued naked outside a bathroom with the bath filled with cold water. At the time, our 'house', Gepps, was being extended and dust screens did not prevent nasty drafts blowing, or indeed itinerant builders from watching events. One by one, using the same water we had to lie in the cold water so the prefect (or indeed on occasion a master) could ensure the water lapped over our shoulders. I still today cannot see the purpose or indeed any educational value of this exercise. I am not sure for how long this continued.

Then, during the 'break' between the morning lessons, we all had to instantly change into gym gear and perform what I thought to be silly exercises in front of the headmasters office.

The next disturbing issue was the compulsory swimming. I gather that my mother had been given a list of clothes items that needed to be labelled with SHA 146 – my number. I still have a coat hanger labelled SHA 146! I can't imagine why I've kept it! I wonder if my mother wondered as to why no bathing trunks were on the list. Yes, you've guessed it. We (i.e. the boys aged 13, 14) had to strip naked, walk around the pool and swim so many lengths. For apparent safety reasons, this was watched by fully clothed prefects and masters on the sidelines. As soon as I could, I stopped swimming.

Then there was the weekly hourly session in the gym. This was scheduled class by class. In my first term, aged 13 and a half, I was, for reasons I still don't understand, in class 5B. This was mainly for fifteen year olds in their fifth year and was the second stream; whilst I could cope well with academic work, the gym was another matter. For example my difficulties with balance and dislike of heights made climbing ropes and vaulting over wooden 'horses' virtually impossible. The gym master was a nasty little muscular bully called Impey who would swing a very hard boxing glove at the end of a cord around his head to gain momentum before hitting his failing gymnast victim. I was clubbed many, many times. Impey also kept telling us that if we wanted girlfriends, we would have to be good at gymnastics. Then he started calling me 'Lucy'.

Then there were sports. Because it was over sooner, I opted for tennis rather than cricket, even though tennis was meant to be 'sissy'.

Athletics gave me nightmares too – quite literally. I was able to run moderately well, but the real problems were the hurdles. My legs were relatively short and I found it difficult to coordinate the taking off jumps from the run. The best I could do was a type of sideways scissors action. We all had to achieve a certain standard for our house. On one occasion, I was made to race on an extra lap on my own.

House order was largely determined by sporting achievements, and I soon sank to the bottom of the house order. Over the years, boys progressed up the house order to the top when they became prefects. I simply could not understand why I should automatically be loyal to an arbitrary allocation to Gepps, particularly as to how I had already been treated. Not surprising, I was on several occasions summoned to the Housemaster, Mr Stephens who did very little teaching. I was accused of having no 'house spirit' and having the 'wrong attitude'.

Among the manifestations of abuse, the rows of toilets were notable. None of them had doors.

The boys also had to participate in silly simulated army games, wearing khaki uniform and drilled by an alleged sergeant major, I think related to gym Impey. The activity tended to be boring and irritating rather than abusive. We paraded outside the infamous school armoury. I did not realise at the time in 1954 that a year before the following happened –

'On 25 July 1953 the schools Combined Cadet Force armoury was raided by the Irish Republican Army (1922–69), making off with 8 Bren guns, 12 Sten guns, an anti-tank gun, a mortar and 109 rifles. Their van was stopped by a police patrol and Cathal Goulding, Sean Stephenson, later known as Sean Mac Stiofain and Manus Canning each received 8 years in prison –

What on earth was the school up to by holding such a stock of weaponry?'

When playing army games, we were referred to as 'Combined Cadet Force'. I do not know with what or whom we were combined.

The army games came to its ironic climax in Thetford Forest, Norfolk, in August 1956. We had the full complement of army uniforms, tents, catering and guns and performing exercises. However, our real attention was diverted to the radio and the Suez crisis leading to the humiliation of the British and French forces, and the resignation of the British Prime Minister, Sir Anthony Eden.

It must have been 1956 when my left knee was hit by a hockey ball causing me to be rested in the school sanatorium for a week. While the swelling slowly subsided, I was bored. A kind nurse lent me a book about discovery of bacteria by a Dutchman in the seventeenth century. Was this the reason for my career in microbiology?

Returning to 1954 after the end of the term, the Lacey family had a wonderful family holiday, driving in an underpowered Singer car via the channel ferry, through France – with one stop – to a village in the Grisons Canton of Switzerland called Bergun. There, life seemed to have stood still for centuries with cattle barns still being an integral part of a human dwelling. I assembled a collection of succulents known as houseleeks, or more correctly, Sempervivums. We did not have a licence to import them, so they were smuggled home!

In September 1954 at Felsted, I was now in class 4A along with other fourteen year old 'swots'. The headmaster whom I had first met at my stammering scholarship interview, had personally made an error (was it deliberate?) by placing me initially in class 5B.

Maybe, I had learnt from life in 5B and would prosper in several subjects notably sciences. I would like to highlight one English lesson. The master was a shortish man, a Mr A. S. M Ronaldson, known unkindly as 'The runt'. The fifty minutes was on logic and its misuse. He covered matters such as circular argument and the fallacies associated with *post hoc, ergo hoc*. I find this valuable to this day. Journalists still seem reluctant to accept that because one relevant incident follows another, it may not have been caused by it.

However, my other English master a Michael Craze was a different matter. He had been glorifying Felsted School in two books and his teaching was mainly pompous dogma. We had to learn by heart the whole of the archaic poem – Lycidas. It was about 180 lines long. We (that is the lower sixth form) were never tested.

In the whole of the year, only one piece of English was marked, and how an end of the year form order was fabricated remains a mystery. However, I was awarded the science prize and the next year the chemistry prize.

Throughout my time at Felsted, there was a huge input of Church of England dogma, with, typically two services daily. I don't think that anyone – be it boys or masters – were anything but bored by the archaic quoting from the bible. The main teacher was the Reverend LSK Ford, nicknamed 'Chinners' that presumably was derived from his large mandible and the favourite word of religious enthusiasts – sinners! Even today the religion of the school is exclusively Church of England. Surely in our multi-cultural, multi-ethnic society there must be proper debate about what, if any is the purpose and function of religion in school. The last fifty years has seen an enormous amount of what I consider reliable understanding of our world and some of the cosmos. The three important areas concern geology and plate tectonics, DNA technology and communication. Criticisms of Darwinian evolution have disappeared. The declining Church of England attendances must raise awkward questions. Have our politicians the courage to generate the debate?

To be positive again, I gained 11 GCSEs (O levels then) including the French oral that I stammered through. My favourite sixth form subject was chemistry and my favourite exercise was identifying the precise nature of an unknown substance.

The chemistry master was JH Lee, a kind man who lived with his family in Felsted village. Because of his voice, he was known as the general. I gained the chemistry prize with a thesis on 'Polymerisation' effectively explaining the details of chemical processes leading to plastics. In the 1950s the prospects of the future use of plastic seemed endless and entirely beneficial. Today, their very success of durability has created an environmental crisis. We (that is all of us) must act over non-essential plastic packaging.

The chemistry master was the figurehead of the school's meteorological society which I had joined in about 1956. We recorded daily various temperatures and measurements of humidity. Some of the thermometers were in a Stevenson screen; others were suspended at depths in the ground.

In 1958, I took and passed the Cambridge entry exam for medicine (first M.B) with A levels a formality. My last few weeks at Felsted were spoiled by two events.

The first involved a tall 18 year old lad who was expelled for possession – of guess what? Answer: condoms that had been used with a cleaner! I bet his parents were pleased with him! At long last, girls entered the sixth form in 1970 and the whole school in 1993. Currently, the annual fees for boarders are £34,275.

My final criticism concerns the geography prize. I had always been particularly interested in winter weather since the winter of 1947. During early 1958, I kept forecast maps and the forecast temperatures in the Times and matched them with the actual temperatures our society recorded and retained. I presented this as an illustrated thesis which was well typed by my father's secretary. I submitted the work some weeks before the end of term, and was waiting for the result to be posted on the notice board.

About three days before the end of term, for some reason, another boy was with the headmaster, when the geography master, a man called Gregory told the headmaster, Henry Reekie, that he had two essays entered for the geography prize, but had not read either. One was presented better (I hope this was mine) than the other. Henry Reekie replied – share the prize between them. The notice to this effect appeared the next day.

It wasn't that I shared the money of the prize that concerned me, but rather the fact he (i.e. Gregory) had not bothered to read it. Goodbye Felsted. I have never been back.

Chapter 3
Cambridge Spies

Before moving 20 miles north to Cambridge, I must include experiences of holidays at my home, 'Squirrels', Little Bardfield. The move from Great Baddow had been carefully planned by my parents being 20 miles from my mother's parents to the north, and 20 miles from Chelmsford and 10 from Braintree. My cat Peter also came and was soon joined by two Siamese kittens to which he presided over with an indifference only a cat can master.

My father's appointment covered rather primitive laboratory tests, unexplained deaths within the hospital and community and the examination of potentially dangerous surgical tissues. Only occasionally was he involved with murders and other incidents usually the responsibility of the 'Home Office Pathologist'. I am quite certain the real life of a pathologist does bear little similarity to that in the detective dramas, even those purporting to be contemporary of this period. I am certain he would not have ventured a detailed cause of death from a cursory inspection of a corpse. He had a reliable assistant called Lincoln who prepared the bodies in a way you won't want to know. He was a keen darts player, and his physique suggested that darts were a good accompaniment to imbibition.

The phone sometimes rang over emergency problems. On answering, it was always, "Great Bardfield 323, Dr Lacey speaking." Only rarely did my father leave the house. His intensive daytime hobby of gardening was rarely interrupted.

In the evening, we would often listen to the radio (I mean wireless), nearly always the BBC home service. We began to play cards as a foursome. Initially whist, followed by bridge would see my younger brother Ian partnering my father with me partnering my mother producing near balance.

Sometimes I created models, electric circuits and motorised vehicles using a silvered girder outfit like Meccano. Then I would construct aeroplanes out of balsa wood, paper and glue from kits. Once to tease my parents, I made a model of a German plane, complete with swastikas. It disappeared during the next school term.

We did not acquire a television until years after the coronation on June 2nd, 1953 that we watched with boredom in Little Bardfield village Hall.

We made our own fireworks. The gunpowder was a mixture of three chemicals readily available from chemists and agricultural suppliers. The containers were glued and rolled paper. The green colour was from barium salts, the red, strontium and the gold sodium. Once, Uncle Brian bought some pure metallic potassium and sodium under oil to prevent self-combustion in air and water. We did not realise the danger until we buried one device and ignited it by pouring water on it. Some neighbours heard the massive explosion and were alarmed. We were safe, but we stopped immediately. Not to be tried at home!

Sometimes my brother and I would drive with my mother in a 1936 Morris 8 to Braintree to buy the groceries. Emphatically then, there was no plastic packaging. The grocer was a friendly shop called 'The International' – a beautiful paradox since nearly all the food was local.

The fishmonger would call on Fridays, and I have never had better fish and chips. My mother coated plaice in breadcrumbs and shallow fried this in fat along with 'our' potatoes.

We had an abundance of eggs in the spring and early summer. Some were preserved in buckets.

My mother was a keen jam maker. The Spanish Seville oranges arriving in January were the essential ingredient in her marmalade. Almost inevitably, my mother became a leading light in the Great Bardfield Women's Institute. She also supported SSAFA, the charity for returning displaced forces personnel.

Sometimes my mother's previous nursing friends would stay, as would my, sometimes, now cantankerous, grandmother (on my father's side).

Other children did not stay! I think my parents thought that such solitude was not such a good idea, although it was of their making. The solution was to send Ian and myself to dancing lessons in the picturesque village of Finchingfield, 5 miles away. It wasn't successful. I didn't take to being manoeuvred by a muscular woman of my mother's age. We went to a few parties at other people's houses; the contrived match-making did not seem to work, and I was still psychologically hurt by events at Felsted. So on going to Cambridge, I felt solitary.

At the end of September 1958, my parents drove me the 20 miles to Cambridge. Despite being still aged 17, the college staff referred to us students as 'gentlemen'; I had a suite of rooms comprising a furnished living room, bedroom, kitchenette and hall. For the first year I was on Chapel Court, and had my own bed maker and cleaner. The college was essentially residential with most of the formal teaching in lecture theatres and laboratories around ¾ miles away. Despite living near the college chapel, I never ventured inside for fear of nasty reminiscence of Felsted.

There were nine other male medical students in college, and we were to become close friends. I found overall that those from day schools were easier to know than the five from boarding schools.

The rules of the college were simple. The outside gates were closed at a precise time and it was essential to sign for a certain number of dinners each term. We (that is our ten medical students) often had a quick half pint of beer in the college bar at the back of Chapel Court, prior to dinner. The college food was much better than Felsted's. There was also a college shop for snacks, drink, toiletries and other essential items. This was called the Buttery. We could run up moderate debt that would provide the stimulus for holiday jobs. I wasn't aware of any rules about what you could do in your rooms, or with whom. The contrast with Felsted was absolute.

Although there was a general requirement to attend lectures, this was rarely a problem because the teaching was excellent, and we were all motivated to become good doctors, although at this stage, no one knew for certain what type.

Anatomy was somewhat different, we had to have our dissections examined and approved by trainee surgeons. For the dissections, each of us had a set of student surgical instruments and a human skeleton that we later would sell to the next generation of students. We never found out the sources of the pickled corpses. Usually two pairs of students would be cutting and probing away on either side of the cadaver. My meetings with the girl students (making up only 15%) occurred in this way. We all wore some protective clothing, making this liaison about as unglamorous as it is possible to achieve.

Doctors, other than surgeons, do have to know the location of the various parts of the human body, at the very least to identify the specialist appropriate for a patient's complaint. For this reason, there was an air of positivity and satisfaction rather than resentment over anatomy. The reason for my reservations about the subject was its static nature, not having evolved since the time of Leonardo de Vinci.

During the first year, some students began polarising towards a career in surgery, but I was thinking along the lines of research and human chemistry.

The opportunities for hobbies and sport were almost infinite. Jesus College had its own cricket ground outside Chapel Court; rowing was a favourite of the college. Amazingly, my sense of balance had improved with my confidence so that I tried canoeing, and could manoeuvre a punt when standing on the rear platform wielding a long pole. I never fell off, not even when passing under many bridges over the river Cam.

I liked the Arts cinema and watched films in black and white from Eastern Europe. Having dabbled a bit in painting at school, I bought and read texts on art and artists. My favourites were early impressionists and those just before.

Many pressure groups jockeyed for your attention. I never understood what 'moral re-armament' was about! One student reading English was approached by what we call now MI6 and was told he was not suitable. This was obviously the case as he had told me about it. Medical students, being committed to their subject do not have this problem. Doctors, I was later to learn, may for example, be approached by the pharmaceutical industry.

One of my favourite pubs was the Fort St. George next to the river on parkland near Jesus College that did own a considerable amount of land and property. It is now the third, most wealthy Cambridge College and has recently undergone a major expansion. Despite this, the college keeps asking for more donations!

One excellent aspect of the Cambridge system is that the term, whether Michaelmas (Autumn), Lent (Spring),or Summer is divisible into 8 weeks of term when all the formal teaching is undertaken and full term of about two weeks either side where most of the university and college facilities remain open. Partly depending on my buttery debt, I sometimes stayed for full term. I would work during the day then play darts or bar billiards in the evening with 'real people' from outside the university. Students were meant to wear distinguishing gowns when out and about at night. I rarely did.

There were neither tuition fees, nor student's loans in those days. My father gave me an allowance that would provide the basics and just a little more. He gave me extra for my eighteenth birthday. A group of us had a meal and 'session' at one of the first Indian restaurants. The prawn curry was nothing like anything I had had before. I can still recall the red flock wallpaper. We were in a small grassed courtyard outside the imposing gates of St. John's College.

I was getting to know other medical students well. Bill had been at a day school in Nottingham, invited me to his parents' house who would kindly purchase later one of my paintings. I liked Goose Fair. Bill had a regular girlfriend in Nottingham but was good at forging friendships with the girl medical students. I can remember watching courting couples surreptitiously under the avenue near Kings College. When one day his girlfriend was on her way, he hadn't any condoms, and felt too awkward to buy them himself, so I did it instead. It was easier to do this for someone else than oneself. Was this the mark of guilt imposed by religion?

Bill became a GP in Jersey and is unfortunately no longer with us.

I had a platonic relationship with a kind girl called Jean whom I treated as an older sister. She was the daughter of a consultant chest physician, in South Essex. I spent a happy weekend with them.

During the second and third years, I lived in the student accommodation in Malcolm Street near Jesus College and a little closer to the town centre. The other students were from famous public schools. They didn't seem to do much work and we didn't get on that well.

During the second year, it was possible to take and, hopefully pass, all the necessary exams to enter clinical (that is seeing patients) medical school and so do a different subject in the third year. The opportunities, freedom and respect at Cambridge were really impressive. So I did this, having to take anatomy twice. My college tutor for anatomy, Dr Bernard Towers, supported my plans, realising that I preferred something more dynamic than anatomy. During the second year, I saw a lot of two other 'old-Felstedians', Chris Wallace and Trevor Culf. Both, like me, were considered swots and not prefect material. We had shared interests in music, and I began collecting one vinyl LP of classical music each week. I am not sure the other students in my lodgings approved of the sound.

So by June 1960, I had passed the necessary exams for clinical medical school beginning September 1961; provided I signed in enough dinners in college, I was assured of a degree and medical progress. So, I had virtually a year 'out'! I tried to get into the Archaeology and Anthropology course, but it was full. I had to settle for Biochemistry. Cambridge had a fantastic reputation for Biochemistry. Watson and Crick (whom Uncle Brian knew) had published their brilliant proposal for the structure of DNA in 1953, the noble prize-winner Fred Sanger was there, so was sugar expert DH Northcote and the head of the department Professor F. G. Young was well known in the field of hormones. Did the teaching match this excellence? No. Most of the lectures were lists of references to works to read, and the practical aspects of 'chemical cookery' were not nearly as interesting as my school chemistry. I gave up attending after two weeks.

I spent much of my time painting. I used hardboard primed with emulsion paint, and after drying did mainly landscapes in oils. I had a few mishaps and had to have my carpet cleaned.

I even had a small exhibition, and was amazed to sell one. Guess who bought it? Amazingly, it was my anatomy tutor Bernard Towers! I have a feeling I owe him a debt to something I don't know about.

During 1960 and 1961, I had been working on a 3 x 4 feet oil painting of my parent's garden. It formed the most obvious picture of the Jesus college art exhibition in June 1961.

Meanwhile, the final examinations for Biochemistry were only three weeks away and I was expected to take the degree exam even having done no recent work. I could not persuade my doctor that I had an anxiety state so went to see my tutor Dr Alan Sharpe. He was an athletic looking man, being an expert on the gas fluorine. I had the distinct impression that he was expecting me. He told me I had to take the exam. Non-attendance at lectures and practicals did not matter. Even failure could give me a pass degree rather than honours. As an incentive he promised a bottle of champagne if I passed.

So for just over two weeks I memorised sections of the subject that could be used within many different types of questions, hopefully marked by different examiners. Unfortunately, when the exam papers came, I knew I was doing very badly.

The last paper came – the general paper that required one three hour answer in one subject area. If a student wrote an essay in a subject he had not done, after 'blind' marking any figure would be doubled for the final assessment.

I still cannot believe my luck. In the Botany section, the subject simply was 'Xerophytes'. These are plants specially adapted to desert or dry conditions; or cacti and succulents.

I was still expanding my collection and propagating the plants at home. I had several books on the subject and was familiar with their Latin genus and species names.

About two weeks later, most of the students who had done biochemistry were awaiting the posting of the results. I don't think many recognised me. Unbelievably, I had passed with good honours second class degree in biochemistry! I can't describe the looks on the faces of some of the students who had spent most of the year doing pointless Laboratory procedures and gained a classification below mine! So on paper, I had a full preclinical qualification in medicine, a science degree and had held a one-man art exhibition. Thank you Cambridge. Just before the end of term my tutor Alan Sharpe called in with a bottle of champagne. He gave me a very strange look.

I decided there and then I would not make the grade as a serious artist.

One thing was still missing from my life – that of a steady girlfriend. Although I had been very enthusiastic about a girl medical student, the feeling was not reciprocated. I was alone.

Observers might have anticipated that with the intermixing of many available nurses and students, I would soon (or rather too soon) become involved and married and it would end in failure. They would be right.

It was usual for students to receive their degree at the formal ceremony. Not liking ceremonies, or liking being the focus of attention, or wanting to dress up like an 18th century headmaster in Priests uniform, I paid a small 'fine' instead. I think my parents were secretly pleased, and I had already had my quiet celebration.

Earlier that year, my father gave me some troubling news, namely that my Aunt Marjorie had been suspended from her post in the Foreign Office after an apparently highly successful career of thirty years. We did not know any details of what her work had been. She had obtained the top first in modern Languages from Newnham College, Cambridge and then entered the Foreign Office. She would now be at home during the summer of 1961, and although this was not discussed openly, I am certain my parents would be interested to know what had happened. It was agreed that I would stay with Marjorie and Charles during July and August of that year.

Charles was the sports editor of the Daily Herald, a paper with socialist sympathies and many of its readers soon would be absorbed into the Daily Mirror. He would telephone his reports in the early evening. His favourite word was 'WHIZZ'. Often, he would be away covering events. He had been a cricketer playing for Essex in the 1930s.

I tried my hand – unsuccessfully – at abstract art and helped in the large and rather chaotic garden. I also observed Marjorie who had two boisterous boxer dogs, after one occasion, returned from a very long walk with her clothes badly ripped and very upset, due, I was told, to a dog fight. Apart from this, the house was peaceful with very few phone calls or visitors. Marjorie was an excellent cook, drank wine moderately, did not smoke, and seemed at the least not to be unhappy. I could never manage the probing of talking about her career and why she had been suspended. The wall of silence was impenetrable.

FIFTY FIVE YEARS ON

In 2016, after the death of a distant relative of my father's mother (maiden name Taylor), another relative, Stuart Hague undertook the work of tracing relatives who might be entitled to a portion of Mrs Elizabeth Madge Rowland's estate. The following had been posted on Wikitree.com on 28/07/2016 by N. Stuart Hague.

'Marjorie worked for MI6 and was Kim Philby's secretary'

In 2017, after the release of some papers relating to the assassination of the then President of the United states of America, JF Kennedy, the following appeared on the BT website last updated 27th October 2017, 12:20, BST.

Cambridge newspaper 'received mystery call just before JFK assassination'.

An anonymous call was made to the senior reporter at the Cambridge News at 6.05pm on the day Kennedy was shot in Dallas, Texas.

A British newspaper received an anonymous call about 'some big news' in America 25 minutes before President John F Kennedy was assassinated, documents have suggested.

The revelation was made in documents relating to the killing, which happened on November 22nd, 1963.

'A memo to the director of the FBI said the anonymous phone call was made to the senior reporter at the Cambridge News on the day Mr Kennedy was shot in Dallas, Texas. The journalist reported receiving the call at 6.05pm, and MI5 calculated it was 25 minutes before the fatal shooting.'

I had some vague memory of my father's family having an association with the Cambridge News; Marjorie, Jack (my father) Brian (Uncle) and Denis (Uncle) had attended the Leys school, a private day school in Cambridge. I looked into this paper claim.

In summary, the Cambridge News was founded and owned by William Farrow Taylor in 1888 whom I now know to be my great grandfather. His daughter Alice Maud Taylor born in 1878 was my grandmother and married Alfred Ernest Taylor in 1907, and Marjorie, full name Alice Maud Marjorie Lacey was born in 1908.

The paper remained in the Taylor/Lacey family up to 1933.

The claims about the phone call have been impossible to verify with my researcher meeting a fair amount of obfuscation. If these allegations were true, the implication would be enormous, but is essentially beyond the scope of this book.

Soon after my stay with Marjorie and Charles, they moved to Spain. Presumably the suspension (if it was actually that) was consolidated into early retirement. My parents visited them at least three times over the decades and did not ascertain any more information. Marjorie and Charles made new friends there and seemed reasonably happy. Charles' sociability balanced Marjorie's reserve.

I now return to the claim that 'Marjorie worked for MI6 and was Kim Philby's secretary. Kim Philby was born four years after Marjorie, obtained a degree in economics at Cambridge, and worked for Soviet KGB from 1934 whilst purporting to be a British agent (spy). In 1935, Marjorie married Douglas Dakin who was born in 1910, and was a lecturer in economics at the London School of Economics. My mother always claimed Douglas was a communist. I do not believe that Marjorie was Philby's secretary in the sense that senior professional people employ staff today for typing, help with the phone and so on. Marjorie was older than Philby and brilliant at modern Languages, not economics.

Moreover in Philby's confessional book 'My Silent War', 1968, there is no mention of Marjorie or a secretary. Is it plausible for a spy representing one country, let alone two, to be accompanied by a confidante during his spy forays? Philby also states that he has not mentioned colleagues or associates still alive.

I consider the more likely involvement of Marjorie at MI6 (known historically as SIS or Secret Intelligence Services) was as recruiter or controller. Marjorie was based in London at this time.

Whilst Philby was apparently cleared of spying by Harold Macmillan in Parliament in 1955, he left his post that year, although it was not until 1962 when George Blake was caught that he was exposed publicly. It is probable that MI6 knew of this pending event a year or so before.

The word 'secretary' can also mean a senior management position within the civil service. The latter could well have applied to Marjorie. When related to spies, the word often used, as stated by Philby's biographer, Philip Knightly is 'controller'. I believe that Marjorie may well have been involved in recruitment or controlling persons such as Philby, and when he was finally exposed her position would have been impossible.

I will make a further point on this matter. That is, during the 1930s, the chief – and possibly all-consuming threat to British national security was from Nazi Germany, and the Soviet Union was an ally, at least in theory. MI6 may well have wanted to recruit people with some understanding of the communist doctrinaire. Obviously, with hindsight attitudes changed. Philby's chief blind spot was the failure to consider our main ally, the U.S.A. I have seen no evidence at all that Marjorie passed any information to another country. She was the absolute archetype of discretion.

James Bond

Kim Philby's biographer, Philip Knightly, states that Philby had charm; he believed that life should be lived to the hilt. Furthermore, women found the mix of idealism and the love of action an almost irresistible combination. Kim had numerous affairs and married four times – a Viennese, an English woman, an American, and a Russian.

Surely, this is the exact character of Ian Fleming's James Bond, but you are questioning how a soviet spy could be the basis of a very British spy? Consider the timing. Certainly up to 1955, and possibly up to 1962, Philby was known to Ian Fleming and others as a British spy. The first James Bond book, Casino Royale was published in 1953, and Fleming could hardly convert a British spy into a masquerading Soviet agent. So I believe Philby was the perfect James Bond prototype.

So was his fictional controller ('M') or Miss Moneypenny based on Marjorie?

Ian Fleming was born in 1908, the same year as Marjorie, and had studied languages in Europe before joining the intelligence services in 1939. Fleming, like Marjorie, was a 'headquarters' person rather than an operative overseas. Therefore, Fleming and Marjorie were similarly trained and experienced, and although wartime detail remain confidential, it would be surprising were they not to have known each other, possibly well.

In 1940, Philby joined SIS (MI6) based in London where Fleming and Marjorie were already employed. During the next few years Philby was responsible for British Intelligence in Spain, Portugal, Italy, North Africa, the Soviet Union and in 1946, Turkey. Fleming left SIS at the end of the Second World War. Philby left the SIS in 1955 because of his association with Guy Burgess. Marjorie remained until 1961.

In Fleming's first James Bond novel, Casino Royale, Bond's controller is described as a man 'M' supported by a secretary Miss Moneypenny who 'would have been desirable but for eyes which were cool and direct and quizzical'. In the early 1967 film based on this book starring David Niven and Peter Sellers, Miss Moneypenny was presented as distinctly glamorous. My father had always described Marjorie as attractive to men. Perhaps this original 'M' and Miss Moneypenny both had some of their character based on Marjorie?

Fleming did have a habit of basing aspects of his fictional characters on actual people. For example, in Agatha Christie's novel published in 1963 and its film adaptation 'A Caribbean Mystery' broadcast on ITV3, 8pm 11/12/17, the name James Bond was randomly picked from a book titled 'Birds of the Caribbean' by an actual James Bond. Both these, James Bond and Ian Fleming were living in the Caribbean in the 1950s, and it would not be surprising if Christie and Fleming had corresponded before Fleming's death in 1964.

One of Fleming's Bond's nemeses can also be attributed to a real person. Henry Blofeld, the well-known sports commentator and raconteur who had played cricket for Cambridge University (inevitably?) states that his father was a student with Ian Fleming at Eton College.

One final thought. If Fleming's James Bond was not derived from Kim Philby, from who was he based?

Chapter 4
Patients

In September 1961, I went to The London Hospital, Whitechapel in East London for the second part of medical training involving patients. In 1990, the hospital became The Royal London Hospital. Ten of us from Cambridge joined about forty students already in London and we were all at the same stage of medical training. There would continue to be some distance between the groups for a year or so. One other Cambridge student was from Jesus College. I shared a flat with Alan, first in Finsbury Park, then in Bethnal Green to be nearer the hospital. I knew Alan well and we had had many arguments about the world population increasing, Alan being a fervent Roman Catholic and defended his church's failure to do enough about it.

Let me make one matter clear. No one is made to take the Hippocratic, or any other oath. However, ethical concerns were always central to our training. Patients were always asked their permission before us students were let loose. If there was any possibility that our involvement might be detrimental to a patient, the procedure did not happen, for example the handling of a possible cancerous swelling. The first few months involved teaching by fairly junior hospital doctors on taking a 'history' that is talking to a patient, including reference to all the bodily functions, mental and social information. Students would write this down in their own section of the patient's notes. It was even sometimes of value for the management of the patient. Instruction of the examination procedure was supported by X-rays and so on. The tricky dilemma, as to when to insert a protected finger into an orifice, was defined. I can recall a leading cardiologist, Wallace Brigden, asking what was harder – taking a good history or performing an 'examination'. Our group said instantly 'examination'. We were wrong.

After our 'induction', we were allocated to join various specialist teams and I noted some of these. We would return to Whitechapel after visiting units and hospitals in East London and Essex, including Chelmsford, after which my father had told me I had made a diagnosis of a new condition 'primary neuronal degeneration'. This might be called Alzheimer's disease today.

In obstetrics, each student was expected to deliver 20 babies. Delivery included attendance during sometimes prolonged labour and the actual delivery would be scrutinised (fortunately for the patients) by midwifes or medical staff. After 13, I gave up, a relief, I think for both patients and staff. This was OK-ed by an affable senior consultant obstetrician called 'Bonzo' Brews. Obstetrics wasn't for me.

In a lecture 'Bonzo' was describing a difficult forceps delivery, when with an absolute impassive face, said, "The difficulty I had getting the thing out, made me wonder how she got in, in the first place." No doubt, rather than the conclusion of pregnancy, I was more interested in its initiation – in the varied meaning.

We had a rather mischievous lecture from Dr Francis Camps, a forensic pathologist, better known as the media-friendly 'home office pathologist' and known to my father. He stressed ways in which doctors could bring about their own downfall by the five As –

ABORTION
ADDICTION
ADULTERY
ADVERTISING
ALCOHOL

He told us that if stopped by police, a doctor who had been drinking should immediately put his head out of the car window to dissipate the fumes! (This was before the breathalyser).

Today in 2018, we could add a few more to these five – murder, unnecessary surgery and unethical drugs trials included.

We spent several months attached to Psychiatric units and saw patients with a range of mental and physical difficulties. I think some of the units relied on students for support. We met patients with severe disability in some mental capacity, but with extraordinary ability in others. We were involved in discussion groups amongst moderately disturbed people. We were residential in Claybury Psychiatric Hospital at Woodford Bridge, Essex. It finally closed in 1997 making way for luxury flats. I wonder what happened to the patients. The hospital in the 1960s appeared to function almost as a self-contained village, with recreational facilities for the staff. I don't think that it had changed much for decades. Then we upset some of the staff. In their bar, open to us, there was an old fashioned one-armed bandit fed by sixpence coins and gravity. The jackpot had not been won for months. We won it. Thirty pounds in 1963 was a major haul. We kept it. Should we have?

I had a problem then with Psychiatry, as I do still. It is not with patients with clear features of say, amentia, dementia, depression and all the major psychoses, neuroses and personality disorders. It concerns the population with slight, uncertain, or intermittent behavioural problems and unable to categorise someone's behaviour as being within normal, or not. There are few objective test criteria that are helpful for these people. It comes down to one parameter – opinion. I can remember being told, "There are as many opinions as there are doctors."

I'll end this unsatisfactory state of affairs by a quote by a fictional Psychiatrist in that wonderful ITV drama, Foyle's War.

"A psychiatrist is a doctor who is trained at great length and expense to persuade others they are mad."

Thank you Anthony Horowitz and Michael Chaplin (series 6, episode 2).

The attachment to the general medical firms was strange. Some of the consultants had their main commitments outside the NHS in the late 1940s and seemed to view the NHS as a duty to suffer. One famous occupational health expert had most of the beds in 'his' ward filled with patients having their blood pressure taken four hourly – and nothing else happened!

The university medical wards contained patients being analysed for precise intake of nutrients and output of waste. This seemed essentially a research endeavour, rather than a procedure to help patients, at least not in the short term.

As with Felsted, I would like to highlight one talk. It was from Dr W. Tegner, a consultant rheumatologist and he told us some of the dangers of the involvement of sectors of the pharmaceutical industry. For example, a doctor might be paid to enter his patients into a trial of a new drug. Some patients would be treated with an old established drug, perhaps to soon lose its financial protection from an expiring patent, so enabling cheap versions (generic drugs) to supplant it. Other patients would receive the new, and, hopefully, better compound. Suppose the new drug was found to be effective – or even more effective – and caused no side effects. Fine. But suppose in some patients, there were side effects and an unscrupulous drug company could find reasons to exclude those patients from the final trial analysis, then adverse effects would be hidden.

It is indeed strange how the true incidence of side effects of drugs is not always identified in early trials. I shall return to this in a later chapter.

Before leaving medicine, we were addressed once by Sir Horace Evans (later Lord Evans) physician to H.M. Queen Elizabeth. He said, "Remember in medicine, the better you do, the more everyone else will hate you."

A general print about the senior consultants, at The London that was worrying us students was their involvement with Freemasonry and their appointment at the Royal Masonic Hospital. The student Christmas show of 1963 included a sketch featuring the Royal Moronic Hospital. I did the scenery.

In surgery, we were not instructed in the performing of minor procedures, such as venepuncture, or setting up infusions or doing needle biopsies. Obviously, we could not experiment on patients, or even ourselves for ethical reasons. We would have to learn the hard way in the future.

My main hobby in the Medical school was chess. I had tremendous battles with other students, Cyrus Kumana and Robert Winston (now Lord Winston) and Mr Webb, an excellent player from the accounts office. I did however, manage to win the London Hospital chess cup presented by a neurosurgeon nicknamed Crackerjack (his true name was Jack Crawford). I did manage to win also, the prize in chemical pathology and diseases of children.

So in June 1964, the ten of us, returned to Cambridge for the final time for the exams. Most of us had already taken and passed a London exam called Conjoint. I suppose we were already doctors. I have never known anyone fail these exams. The main problem for the examiners (mainly consultants) is to find patients with disorders that a succession of students can attempt to diagnose there and then. These volunteer patients did receive a fee, and their helpful intent often favoured the student rather than the examiner. One patient would show the student his diagnosis on a piece of paper when concealed from the examiner. I think some students believed they should have exchanged roles with the examiner!

In practice, the ten students from Jesus College all knew we had passed and treated the occasion as a reunion party. We were staying in college, and I have a vague memory of climbing over the railings to get back in.

Doctor Richard Westgarth Lacey now returned to London and bought a new car – a white Hillman Imp registered EN0 490B and not the most reliable of experimental designs. It would soon be spending the autumn of 1964 and the following winter stored in the barn at Squirrels.

I did a research job at The London Hospital during August and then it happened on September 1 – my first day as a junior hospital doctor. It started with a bang. No further training, no induction and no advice. The work was in general surgery with an emphasis on the treatment of bowel cancer. I was responsible for planning operating lists, assisting either consultant surgeons in operating theatres, admission of patients, taking their general medical histories, their general examinations, writing and updating their notes, prescription of drugs, their post-operative care and finally their discharge.

If I had problems, I could seek help from the team's trainee surgeons – Jack Hardcastle, the Registrar and Charles Mann the senior Registrar. Both would become distinguished surgeons in their own right. As with other juniors, the main problem I experienced was setting up drips (technically infusions) and other practical procedures.

The senior ward nursing staff was extremely helpful and must have been satisfied with all their junior doctor pupils who they discretely and sensitively guided. I was far too busy to even question as to whether or not I was happy. I recall having just two afternoons off in six months; during one I had a haircut and fell asleep. Otherwise I was on-call continuously. At night, the telephone would ring frequently, mainly for me to authorise drugs for patients, usually sleeping aids (for them, not me).

On Sunday mornings, I accompanied one consultant on his trip around his private patients to enact required changes in drug therapy and general 'housekeeping' matters. He gave me a generous cheque at the end of the six months. There seemed to be an overlap between private patients in their private single rooms, and 'amenity' type patients in single rooms within formal NHS territory. I had no evidence of impropriety.

One aspect of surgery involving incision through the bowel that caused concern was the possibility of bacteria becoming implanted into an area of the body that were normally bacteria-free (sterile) and causing infections such as peritonitis. For this reason, patients at risk, including all patients about to undergo surgery on the colon and rectum were given by mouth large doses of antibiotics prior to the operation.

After surgery, the consultant would usually ask me to give the patient post-operative antibiotic 'cover', leaving the choice of drugs to me.

In the 1960s, largely due to the forceful opinions of one man – L.P. Garrod – it was thought that the administration of two antibiotics simultaneously would reduce the risk of bacteria becoming resistant. Ten years later I would challenge this vehemently, and years later, successfully. However, at this time in 1964, my patients received two antibiotics when, with hindsight one, or even none would have sufficed.

I am afraid that in this next section, I cannot avoid being somewhat anatomical and technical. So be warned. Most cancers of the colon occur in the lower part just prior to the rectum that ends in the anus. A considerable number of cancers occurred in the rectum itself. The purpose of the surgery was to remove the segment of the bowel containing the cancer and rejoin the ends of the healthy gut left behind to produce in time normal – flowing gut contents. The problem relates to when the rejoining cannot be achieved because cancer was too near the anus. There were various procedures that could be tried such as the 'pull through' when it was hoped the colon would unite with the anus. However, sometimes the only solution would be to divert the colon to the front of the abdomen as a colostomy.

My two surgeons had different approaches and indeed expertises, and also fully discussed the options with the patients. Where the cancer was in the critical location in the rectum near the anus, one surgeon would remove the tumour and create a colostomy in the fairly speedy operation. The other surgeon would often do two operations, with the first creating a temporary colostomy, followed by a second operation rejoining the bowel. Since the second approach would involve two operations, there was more risk of matters going wrong, but many would not have a permanent colostomy.

My point of troubling you with these details is that they illustrate the futility of simple targets and statistics imposed by those ignorant of medical procedures. I am not impressed by the lack of input of medical members of parliament into the creation of our target society. I am sure this applies also to teaching and any under-resourced service, and does transfer the blame for failure from the politicians to the individual. I believe that many other aspects of patient's care have been reduced to the minimum dictated by targets, and as the money runs out, politicians stuck in their own dogma, the quality of life under the contemporary NHS continues to fall. I shall return to this later.

I did perform 'minor' operations under supervisions, including an appendicectomy, a hernia repair and a removal of a lipoma – an aggregate of non-cancerous fatty cells. Then a tricky moment happened. Our operating theatre was the last to finish, and the junior trainee surgeon had been called to a ward emergency. This left me and the senior consultant to finish the last operation. The consultant suddenly left, saying to me, "You finish off!" The trouble with wearing masks and protective gowns is that it can obscure your identity. Presumably, the consultant thought I was the training surgeon rather than the junior House Officer – my actual status. So with firm and diplomatic guidance from the theatre nurse sister and anaesthetist, I managed to stitch up the large abdominal wound, making sure there were no instruments or gauze swabs left in the abdomen. During the next few days, the patient must have wondered why I visited him so much! He was fine. In writing up the notes, I put the names of the surgeon as the consultant and mine!

In those days, anaesthetists were provided by a very skilled group of doctors who were not quite as subservient to the surgeon as might be thought. Often the type and length of the surgery would be influenced by an anaesthetist. The enormous advances in the precise timing of the anaesthetic have been a major factor in improving surgical outcome. The skills needed are very impressive. Anaesthetists don't quite receive the public acclaim they deserve.

One consultant anaesthetist tried to recruit me to his ranks, but I knew surgery was not to be my ambition. In later years, I produced a humorous definition on a slide for general practitioners; 'A consultant is a person who thinks his speciality is more important than anyone else's'.

What a six months 'baptism' (is that the right word?) to the real medical world! Would the next post be a type of holiday that I thought I should experience? Not quite.

The second house officer post from March 1965 was in paediatrics with responsibility for ill new born babies, young patients on the ward, sometimes seeing children in casualty (still described as the receiving room). It was whilst here as a student, I had first heard of J. F. Kennedy's murder, and being unaware that my family had owned the Cambridge News and its subsequent strange report.

I was also responsible for giving a check on the babies born at home in the East End of London, for dislocation of hips, heart abnormalities and so on. I am pleased to say that all the babies were healthy and it was interesting to see inside their homes.

I can remember my father telling me that when he was a young GP in Burley-In-Wharfedale, he was asked to judge a 'baby contest'. He gave the prize to the prettiest mother!

As with surgery, I was answerable to two consultants, one in his late thirties, Anthony Jackson, and one, around sixty, Richard Dobbs who often teased Dr Jackson using his wealth of experience. There were also two trainee registrars on the ladder to becoming consultant paediatricians. Unlike surgery, prescriptions for drugs and the requests for tests were carefully controlled by the registrars. I was the scribe who was learning.

The senior consultant owned a Jaguar saloon similar to that driven by fictional detective Morse, I felt important on being taken to see patients – sometimes private – in their home.

There were numerous discussions and so called case conferences with social services over babies and children that may or may not have been abused by their parents or others. There was a true built-in professional need to distinguish between accidental and what was called non-accidental damage. When matters go wrong, it is easy for inquiries to lay blame with hindsight. But at the time we would consider very carefully all the facts and try not to stigmatise a family unnecessary, nor to fail to protect a baby or child from further injury. Seeing their family in the home was valuable for the doctors, as was the presence of social workers in hospital. The whole procedure was very labour intensive, and I am not sure that retrospective inquiries always understood the pressures at the time.

My concerns were sometimes alerted in casualty when an infant was brought in by his or her father, or more distant relative. I don't think we made any major errors. If we had, presumably we would have been lambasted by the media?

Perhaps, the most difficult aspect of the job was to talk to parents about a child who was unlikely to recover, or even worse, had died. Fortunately, this was rare.

By the summer of 1965, I began thinking about my career, realising that I had no formal experience of adult medicine (as opposed to surgery) and I also wanted a break from London.

In September 1965, now aged 24, I began working for two consultant physicians and one consultant paediatrician at St. Mary's Hospital Eastbourne. There were no medical registrars and I had more responsibility than in London for day to day prescriptions, tests and making liaisons for discharge.

Many of the adult patients had stomach ulcers – not known then to be mainly due to infections. Some patients had asthma, some had had heart attacks, and others had 'PUO'. This is medical shorthand for pyrexia of unknown origin or 'the patient has a temperature and the doctor does not know why'. I found these patients an interesting challenge as a common cause is a type of infection, and this would lead me to my ultimate speciality – microbiology.

One feature showed by many adult patients in Eastbourne was depression. Not that the depression caused the specified non-psychiatric condition, but the patients awareness of his or her symptoms was amplified. Many of the depressed patients had retired to the south coast from industrial towns of the North of England and were missing their family and friends. On a grey and windswept winter's day, the seafront at Eastbourne is not quite a paradise!

Without medical registrars, the junior doctors, or housemen, were reliant on senior nursing staff for help and advice. Certainly for the management of life-threatening crisis, the male and female staff was more valuable than inexperienced doctors. With nursing becoming a high technology university-based discipline, I am not sure who fills this role now (2018), or who provides the compassionate dimension to patient care.

The missing registrar posts were illustrated by one occasion when my consultant physician had an acute illness and could not see about 12 patients referred by GP's in outpatients. So I 'acted up' quite literally as a consultant. I managed to refer some to other consultants, a few to x-rays and tests and a return appointment, when hopefully my consultant had passed his kidney stone (very painful).

By early 1966, I knew what I wanted to do – become fully trained in general pathology and then specialise in one branch. When my father had trained in pathology in the 1940s a consultant was responsible for all aspects, except perhaps public health. By the 1960s, general pathology had been divided into four different specialists – histopathology, haematology (diseases of the blood), chemical pathology (laboratory tests), microbiology (scientific basis of infection). The first two years would be spent on learning all four branches, then hopefully, pass an exam before doing specialist training in one for three years prior to the final exam. Research was encouraged.

I applied for a training post in Bristol and was accepted from September 1966.

One final point at the St. Mary's Hospital concerned patients of the consultant chest physician. Previously, accurate and reliable research from Oxford (I hate to admit!) had shown that cigarette smoking could cause lung cancer. Many patients with the possible or probable disease were being seen and admitted, sometimes into beds normally identified for other specialists. Indeed, this seemed to be the first NHS 'bed crisis' and was aggravated by injuries over the Christmas celebrations. We did, however, manage the problem. It is quite remarkable how attitudes about smoking were beginning to change. My father had given up completely, but my mother couldn't (or wouldn't?).

Around 2016, I acquired a copy of the Black Cat album for postage stamps of the world, published by the tobacco company Carreras, London, in 1905. The album contained much promotional material and quoted support from the prestigious medical journal, the Lancet, many scientists and the appointment of the company to the royal family. There was specific endorsement from J.M. Barrie, a GP who had written in his work 'My Lady Nicotine' concerning Carreras Craven mild, the following:

'It is deliciously mild, yet full of fragrance, and it never burns the tongue. If you try it once you smoke it ever afterwards. It clears the brain and soothes the temper. When I went away for a holiday anywhere I took as much of that exquisite health – giving mixture as I thought would last me the whole time, but I always ran out of it. Then I telegraphed to London for more, and was miserable until it arrived. How I tore the lid off the container! That is a tobacco to live for.'

Barrie is clearly describing a drug addiction for which he is unable to plan! Let us remember him for the delightful and fanciful Peter Pan, rather than a pawn for the tobacco industry.

In the 1960s any doctor who has qualified and undertaken a year's 'housejobs' as a junior Doctor was eligible for general practice. Not surprising, out of interest and as an extra income, many doctors in training posts did locums for GP's on holiday. Over the next five years, I suppose I must have done about six month's general practice in total. The newly qualified locum has the advantage of knowing recent medical changes, but is ignorant of local and family matters.

I had a few awkward episodes. I gave a young woman a sickness note for a cold. I wrote URTI on the form, standing, of course, for upper respiratory tract infection. Thirty minutes later she rushed into my room with two other girls, shouting, "I know what you have written – URTI – stands for 'you are too idle'!" If the cap fits, wear it!

On another occasion, about thirty minutes after the surgery should have closed (there were no appointments then) a women came in with four children, with the youngest seemingly vandalising the room's contents. After asking her who the patient was, she smiled sweetly and replied, "All of us," and proceeded to request a whole series of letters and notes barely within medical relevance. With the youngest, I mentioned he could do with a smack, meaning it metaphorically. I had a mild formal rebuke from the then 'Executive Council', whoever they were.

After many surgeries, I would undertake as many as ten home visits either as planned 'follow-ups' or for patients who found it difficult to attend the surgery. Then the routine workload of the GP was much less than now. Half of the then smaller aging population were not on regular drugs that needed to be monitored. It is simply not possible for this number of home visits to be undertaken today (2018). No wonder so many patients resort to casualty attendance. I think many observers await more studies that are truly independent of the pharmaceutical industry of the impact of long term therapy to lower cholesterol and blood pressure. My instinct is that we (that is society) have been following the wrong road up an endless cul-de-sac?

My favourite locum venue was over the Severn Bridge to Dr John Battle in Coleford in the Forest of Dean. The surgery was part of a wonderful house, with lawned gardens down to a stream. He had his own dispensing pharmacy, and was looking forward to retirement. I could have accepted his offer for me to take over the house and practice. I didn't for two reasons. My domestic lifestyle was not settled and I had other ambitions. *So should I have taken up this offer?* I wonder.

Was this goodbye patients?

Not quite.

Chapter 5
Back to Basics

In March 1966, I joined the junior doctors at Bristol Royal Infirmary as a promoted senior house officer. This post was for a year prior to moving up to registrar for basic training in all branches of pathology. Taking my turn with three other trainees, I would be resident one night in four to do the emergency tests; examples were to ensure patients would receive the safe transfusion blood, glucose levels for diabetics with problems, and fluids from patients with suspected meningitis. We had been instructed by skilled laboratory technicians who would later be redefined – correctly – as 'Medical Laboratory Scientific Officers' MLSO's. These, in many ways replaced nurses as the new mentors. If we ran into problems over performing the tests, an emergency MLSO was always available.

I lived initially within one of two general practices, and did the occasional surgery. The atmosphere and morale among the junior doctors as a group was optimistic; in our lounge there would normally be a card group revelling in playing bridge. This was lead mainly by the radiology juniors still preoccupied by x-rays, and a small input of ultrasounds. Radiology had not become 'imaging' yet and the trainees had ample leisure time. As a group of young doctors, we knew we were at the sharp end of rapid developments in medicine. The topic of conversation often turned to prospects abroad, particularly in the U.S.A. In training, we had received free university education for 5 or 6 years and were then receiving paid medical training for a further similar period.

I was concerned about the ethics of this. However, many colleagues and friends did achieve excellent posts abroad. California was probably the favourite destination. The media had dubbed this the 'Brain Drain'. The Labour government under the

Huddersfield – born Prime Minister, Harold Wilson was clearly concerned, and I would benefit later directly from this.

My new consultant bosses included Professor William Gillespie, a kind and clever Dubliner who had many national and international commitments. One morning, a slightly disgruntled consultant physician was seeking William (how we always referred to him) as were the trainees. Joe Cates said to us, "What is the collective noun for professors?"

Answer: "An absence."

One of the highlights of the first year was a course on statistics by the erudite and amusing Miss Duncan. I will always be impressed by this story. In the 1960s, it was almost impossible to buy any goods without free stamps. Green shield stamps were endemic! The abundant petrol was being sold with half simulated money notes, and if both halves of say a 20 pound note were collected, then the payout would be due. After statistical advice, the cost of the fuel was adjusted to allow for the rare occasions when two halves were combined. Unfortunately, for the petrol company, the possibility of advertising by the holders of one half of a high value token had not been considered. The advice that should have been given was that print only a very, very small number of one side of high value tokens. So in a batch, instead of printing 10 left and 10 right £20 tokens, print just 1 left and 19 right. The moral: statistics are only as valid as the relevance of the study.

I think I was beginning to understand the principles of studies and research that I will summarise now.

Identify a problem that interests you.

Perform thorough readings, and ideally your colleagues, unit or department are involved in similar.

Perform experiments, surveys or trials that are relevant, and have reliable and reproducible measurements.

Cut out any possibility of human bias.

Never begin a project with an intent to prove anything (that is your personal prejudice). Instead set out by asking the question 'whether or not…'

Consider whether your findings can be applied generally.

During a series of experiments avoid changing more than one variable at a time. Otherwise you will not know which change caused the effect, and you will have to repeat the experiment anyway.

Even by using the best statistical model, differences in sets of results are said to be significant if they are likely to occur at an incidence of less than one in twenty. For example if 50 random tests for body chemicals produced three results outside the normal range, this could be deemed significant, whereas 2 would not; very arbitrary. Cynics say that statistics are only required if the findings are in doubt.

Finally, do not let financial sponsors have the ability to alter or suppress publication of your findings.

So I thought I knew how to do research; but on what?

Before going into details, an incident happened in 1967 for which I am not proud, but extremely fortunate.

Soon after the breathalyser came into force in 1967, I went to a party with a person who I thought was my 'partner'. I suppose girlfriend might have been a better term then. Many people were there who I did not recognise. We were shown a series of home videos including, what today might be called hard porn. After this, my partner disappeared as did another man. I think I must have had one or two drinks too many because on driving home at the first T-junction, I demolished a lamppost, sending it over and blocking a fairly main road in Downend.

I was still confused when a passing car stopped; the driver moved the lamppost and took me home to Yate. The police arrived next morning, but did not breathalyse me. I shall always owe that person eternal thanks. Incidentally, the name of the public house near the pathology department at the back of Bristol Royal Infirmary was named 'The Good Samaritan' from which we could be available on-call. I had learnt a lesson. I never took such a risk again.

So what took my interest for research? Whilst at Cambridge an erudite tutor D. G Fulton Roberts, a consultant haematologist had read us a poem titled 'The battle of *furunculosis*. This refers to a collection of pus in the skin due to a bacterium called *Staphylococcus aureus*. The word *Staphylococcus* comes from Greek and means a collection of spheres arranged like a bunch of grapes, and *aureus* is Latin for golden colour because of the appearance of large groups of bacteria when grown artificially on the surface of nutrient gels.

Fortuitously, the main research interest of the microbiology unit at Bristol Royal Infirmary, headed by William Gillespie and Dr George Alder, an eminent scientist was the *Staphylococcus* and the problems it was causing. The reputations were international, and the group, with full support of clinical staff had shown that spraying antibiotics onto the body surface of patients was particularly liable to cause and spread these bacteria that were resistant to antibiotics.

Many people have heard the term MSRA. This is short and for methicillin resistant *Staphylococcus aureus*. Methicillin, is not now used as an antibiotic, but resistance to it means resistance to all the penicillin-type antibiotics (called beta Lactams) and also too many other types.

Partly due to the work already performed at Bristol, much was known about the natural history of SA (by which I shall now refer *Staphylococcus aureus*). SA resides – usually harmlessly – in moist regions of the human body, particularly in the nose, around the groin, armpits, but not the eyes.

On any one occasion, around a third of the population harbour SA in their nose unwittingly and innocuously. The fear of SA spreading from patients nostrils to surgical wounds explains the routine procedure of swabbing patient's noses prior to surgery. Hopefully, the surgeons and other attendants are also checked! (What about visitors, you may wonder!)

Inevitably, SA would spread by usual human activity from moist regions to dry skin, where it was thought to succumb by acids on the skin surface. My research, then guided by William and George would attempt to study the death of SA on the forearm skin of genuine volunteers – doctors and scientists. The numbers of SA applied were very small, the strains of SA used were sensitive to many safe antibiotics, and during the experiments no one acquired a skin infection. I wonder if ethical approval had been needed today, would it have been granted.

Since this series of experiments, I have volunteered for many research projects. I only had a problem with one. It was over ten years later; I took a normal dose of lithium over weeks for psychiatrist colleagues. Whilst I thought I was psychiatrically fine before the drug, I was feeling odd on treatment, my voice almost coming to a standstill during a lecture.

It took me some time to perfect a sampling method for the skin testing. I found the best way was to use gummed paper labels. They were sterile and glue was ideal to transfer the bacteria from the marked forearm skin areas onto the surface of nutrient gels. As the labels were repositioned on the gel serially, the numbers of bacteria deposited fell, and the counts gave the relative survivals.

When considering whether particular strains of SA might be better or worse at skin survival, I developed a method of using mixtures whereby differences in the golden hue enables various test strains of SA to be compared to a constant lemon-coloured standard. Because the acidity of the human skin was due to fatty acids, I tried the effect of washing with soap, ethyl alcohol and the powerful fat solvent, acetone.

The first results were published in the British Journal of Experimental Pathology in 1968. In summary, there were no big differences between the varying strains of SA. Antibiotic resistance did not enhance survival. However, after washing with soap (containing no antiseptic) SA survived better, after alcohol swabbing much better, and after acetone even more so. High humidity also increased the persistence of SA on the skin.

After this work was published in 1968, I had a letter from scientists working in San Francisco, wanting me to do further work on prison inmates. This would not have involved prisoners in Alcatraz that shut in 1963. The American system of science, medicine and pathology was quite different to ours, there being no 'Medical Microbiologists'. So I declined the invitation. I am certainly pleased now I did.

Some years later, the Times literary supplement featured this work referring to me 'As the Great unwashed'. It is interesting that the mass use of soap by *Homo sapiens* is a very recent development in our evolution, and little research into the impact has been undertaken.

The problem raised by our department previously had been the spread of resistant bacteria associated with the use of the antibiotic neomycin. So I went back to basics – quite literally. Neomycin is a basic chemical in that it contains free amino groups and produces an alkaline solution. The free fatty acids were acidic because of their carboxylic groups. Basic and acidic molecules have the potential for chemical union. Indeed there was already a commercially used derivative of neomycin as a result of this union. I found that basic neomycin molecules could indeed precipitate with fatty acids of the sort found on the skin.

The next stage was for me cautiously to treat one arm with neomycin, with the other untreated as a control. Cultures of SA resistant to neomycin were then applied and the arms sampled about 5 hours later. When the conditions were right, the treatment with neomycin did indeed encourage the persistence of SA.

Problem solved? Not quite. The consultant dermatologists did not seem to want to know and publication of results was extremely difficult.

However, all the experimental details and reviews of the literature and skin sampling methods comprised a thesis for a Cambridge Doctorate of Medicine that was successful despite a somewhat aggressive oral examination. I don't think dermatologists are too enamoured with microbiologists. This was my fifth Cambridge degree, and I say again: Thank you Cambridge. Is Prince William due for an honorary doctorate?

It seems that in 2018 hydrating or moisturising cosmetics have reached almost epidemic proportions. I suppose they are less undesirable than those containing tiny plastic spheres that can damage marine life. What on earth are we doing with plastics?

Three events happened in 1968. First, I took and passed the first part of the Royal College of Pathologists, specialising in microbiology and chemical pathology. I bought my first house, having been saving with an insurance company for two years. My father's mother had recently died and left me £500 of her Cambridge News booty. I borrowed £4250 of the £5250 agreed price. In 2000, the Daily Telegraph very kindly did a feature on this house with me and had it valued then £300-330,000!

Kings cottage was in the village of Didmarton nearly opposite the King's Arms near the southern edge of the Cotswolds close to Badminton, 20 miles from Bath and Bristol, and 8 miles from Tetbury. Not far away was my idea of paradise – not Highgrove, but Westonbirt Arboretum. There were several delightful nearby villages such as Sopwirth, Luckington and Sherston. Sometimes on Sundays I would intermingle with local young farmers in Malmesbury who really hated the Labour Prime Minister, Harold Wilson.

This was the heart of conservative England lead by the Duke of Beaufort's Hunt in Badminton. On two occasions, we hid the fox in our garage. There were few shops still open in the local villages and many of the cottages were weekend retreats. Society was beginning to change. I came to know the Duke's head of forestry well, a charming old dear called Charley. The Landlord of the King's Arms was a retired policeman and a sing song with accordion was given by council staff most Saturdays not to uniform acclaim.

The third event of 1968 was the creation of a new post of Lecturer in Clinical Microbiology, one of Harold Wilson's attempts to retain costly young doctors in this country, and the post meant moving from the dungeons at the back of the Bristol Royal Infirmary to the newish purpose-built university building. I also had a room in the Laboratory of the children's hospital just opposite my university room, both at the top of St. Michaels Hill. Apart from being required to give, perhaps 20 lectures a year to medical and dental students, I devoted the next few years to basic research. We worked as several separate teams at the university. Colleagues included John Grinsted, Ian Chopra, and John Anderson, all meticulous scientists. I learnt from them and provided ideas and the patient relevance, in addition to the bacteria.

As a unit, the microbiology department at Bristol University had a wide interest in many aspects of infections, notably antibiotic resistance. The key breakthrough in this field had occurred in the 1950s, when Japanese workers showed that resistance to several antibiotics had passed simultaneously from one type of bacterium to another in patient's intestines. This was indeed by a type of sexual activity in these bacteria, called conjugation. A number of dreadful jokes abounded about the need for bacterial contraceptives!

The Americans – as is often their want – confirmed and extended this work and had begun to study how the genes for antibiotic resistance might spread in *Staphylococcus aureus* (SA). This was led by the brilliant Richard Novick from New York in the 1960s.

The idea was that most strains of SA had one or more 'resident' viruses comparable to human nerve cells and the shingles virus. Bacterial viruses are known as bacteriophages, from the Greek meaning literally bacteria – eaters because occasionally the phages do destroy their host, releasing many copies of the virus. Sometimes piece of DNA from the host bacteria is inadvertently (it seems) incorporated into the phage that on infecting a new SA cell transfers that extra piece of DNA in a small coiled circle called a plasmid. If the extra DNA carries genes for antibiotic resistance, then transfer of resistance would have occurred. The process must be very inefficient because the potential donor bacteria would be destroyed and most of the potential recipients also by the predominant 'normal' phage's.

I began the research by taking random SA from patients and mixing them together to see what happened. For example if one SA was resistant to antibiotics A and B, another was resistant to C and D, I would identify (the scientific term was 'select') bacteria resistant to A and C, A and D, B and C. Then I would try and identify the direction of the transfer. I expected transfer to be rare. It often was. But not infrequently, the transfer rate was very high – as high as that been gut bacteria, say E. *coli* and shigella.

It took me some time to find out what was happening. It was exciting work, and I would be in my laboratory all hours of the day and night. The cell of SA has a rigid wall and I couldn't see how a type of conjugation was occurring. I was certain that the phage was involved. I took a standard culture of SA (I still recall its number of 1030) and inserted one of about twenty different phage's into each cell, to be followed by one of several plasmids I knew to be capable of transferring antibiotic resistance into further derivatives. Matters were becoming very complicated, so I'll skip to the conclusion: the key for ease of transfer was not the phage on the donor, but its presence in the potential recipient. So the current problem with MRSA was indeed due to the sequential acquisition of new DNA plasmids from other SA, and selected by antibiotic use in patients. I did show that this process could also occur on the skin of volunteers. However, my job changed and I could not follow this up. I hope others have.

Around 1970, we began looking at different sources of MRSA indentified and stored over the years. All seemed to have a common core set of properties with variable additional antibiotic resistance, presumably a reflection of the antibiotic use at the time. We believed that they were of one cell line or 'clonal'.

It is easy to see how such a varied group of SA could arise when, under perfect conditions, a new generation can emerge 'every twenty minutes'! With bacteria, since the beginning of the antibiotic era in the 1940s, we have watched evolution occur on a massive scale and the idea of continuous slow and minor change enabling survival of the fittest is only partly true, we must add the phenomenon of large and abrupt evolution. I think Charles Darwin himself might have been accepted that he had understated the theory.

In 1970, I had received a research grant from the Cystic Fibrosis Research Trust to look at details of SA in children with this illness. The work was undertaken at Bristol Children's Hospital. I was very ably helped by Evelyn Lewis. We would test many hundreds of cells of SA from sputum samples, looking for both sensitive and resistant derivatives. We were to find that even during therapy some bacteria sensitive to the drug could be found. And when that agent was replaced, the proportion resistant SA to be the first drug dropped over the ensuing months. Antibiotic resistance appeared to be reversible.

Meanwhile I was playing God, creating a 'superbug' by inserting up to 6 different plasmids into one SA bacterium. On cultivation in the laboratory, the superbug looked identical to its parent SA when grown in the absence of antibiotics. At this time there were no statutory controls to prevent 'escapes' of superbugs. This would soon change.

Then I did the nearest procedure to an animal experiment in my life. This involved inoculating incubated fertile hens eggs to see how the virulence (its ability to destroy the embryo) of the superbug compared to the control (or wild) SA. No permission or animal licence was needed. The procedures were blind and randomised and I was helped by several colleagues. No doubt, the superbug was less virulent than the wild.

Then in other experiments, I tested the superbug to find out whether or not the resistances persisted without antibiotic exposure (i.e. selection pressure). Some resistances persisted better than others, but there was a general trend for the SA to revert to the wild in the absence of antibiotics. I published to this effect and had some hostility from the pharmaceutical industry. The industry seemed to want to be presented as the good guys ridding us of evil bacteria intent on destroying people. Any antibiotic resistance would create the need for new 'magic bullets' often to replace the older drugs not now covered by commercial patent protection.

Sometimes, the experiment had failed due to errors or equipment difficulties. I was pleased to have the regular job of overseeing the microbiology unit at the Children's Hospital. The atmosphere was very good. The consultant haematologist, Dr Alan Raper was a charming, if diffident gentleman who looked at many of the blood films of ill children himself. Leukaemia, as I found in Eastbourne, was a serious matter with treatment still often unsuccessful. My future wife for 32 years, Fionna, was a scientist in haematology and favoured the mini skirt. She was a redhead from Edinburgh and had spent the last three years in Canada.

On one occasion in 1972 Fionna's parents had been staying with us at King's Cottage. Her father, David had said, "It's about time you made an honest woman of my daughter." He used to refer to me as 'Tricky Dicky' after Richard Nixon. So, knowing my dislike of formal ceremonies, and knowing there might be awkwardness with our families, I secretly booked a Registry Office wedding in Bath.

The evening before, I asked Fionna to get married. She said, "Yes."

So I said, "It's tomorrow."

It was.

At this time, Bristol was booming and had been catching up the London enthusiasm. I liked the Berni Inn Restaurants, and prawn cocktail followed by fried bread crumbed plaice, chips and peas will always be a favourite. The whisky-fuelled TV food raconteur Keith Floyd was indulging nearby. On one occasion, I went to a restaurant believing the meat to be pheasant until a zoological colleague announced loudly the skeleton was a rabbit!

Fionna and I began to furnish King's Cottage with second hand furniture and antiques bought from auctions and dealers. Then our objective was to remove inappropriate paint and varnish that was obscuring the natural grain of the wood. It is amazing how the contemporary fashion in 2018 has changed full circle.

Back to work, I was giving honorary (unpaid) lectures on medical matters to the biochemistry students up the hill at the University of Bath. I think knowing some basic biochemistry should be included in all basic education and indeed in particular for the pedlars of gimmick dieting formulae. Why has not anyone told them that eating excess protein, carbohydrate – or anything – is converted into body fat? I subscribe to Dr Philip Hammond's philosophy – to lose weight, eat smaller portions. That is all that is needed.

I suspect my lectures then were a touch boring, feeling the need to cover all the aspects of the subject. At the time, the course convenor (that is boss) for the medical students, William Gillespie produced a booklet for each student with each lecturer supplying a several page summary of each talk. I never liked this 'spoon-feeding' and thought it might damage interest and attendance in the subject. I thought then that the booklet was an intended benefit for the students, but I wonder now as to whether its principle intent was to improve the competence of us junior lecturers. Incidentally, never did I ever have any training in lecturing.

The nearest I came to advice was when an antibiotic whiz-kid colleague David Reeves told me my slides should have been 'blue' not black.

By 1973, I was teaching and tutoring science students in addition to medical and dental, but felt I did not quite have the 'scientific' authority. So I submitted published work under the general heading 'Transferable Antibiotic Resistance in *Staphylococcus aureus*' to the University of Bristol and received a Doctorate of Philosophy. Previously, I had obtained the Diploma in Child Health in 1966 and had passed the final of the Royal College of Pathologists in 1971. No wonder, my science head accused me of suffering from 'diplomatosis'.

In 1973, the University of Bristol promoted my lectureship to Reader in Clinical Microbiology. Thank you Bristol. However, my clinical grade was only senior registrar – still a trainee. I was offered one half day a week as a very part time consultant. Outrageous. I wasn't sure who I had upset, but I would find out soon.

63

Meanwhile, in addition to research on SA, our attention (mainly with John Anderson who ended up in Vancouver) turned to the basic errors in the concept of co-trimoxazole. This had been marketed in 1968 and consisted of a mixture of sulphamethoxazole (SUL) and Trimethoprim (TRI), allegedly combined to enhance potency and prevent the formation of resistant bacteria. Its trade names were Septrin and Bactrim. Strictly, these substances were not antibiotics, but antibacterial agents, being entirely synthetic. Sulphonamides were developed for the dye industry in 1935, and TRI was a compound similar to those moderately successful in treating some human cancers.

Performing similar experiments as the makers had quoted; we did find that the two drugs did reduce the incidence of resistance as claimed. But (and this is a very big but) the resistant mutants grew very slowly, had severe metabolic damage and would not be expected to cause disease. Indeed, some of the resistant mutants actually required these antibacterials to survive, so the bacteria would succumb when the drug was withdrawn! This phenomenon was well known at the time and was called 'dependence'.

It was known in the 1960s that antibiotic resistance in naturally – occurring bacteria was due to proteins containing a precise order of amino acid sub units. These could not arise out of nothing from a single laboratory procedure. In order to support the idea that the two drugs would prevent, resistance, the microbiologists of the time, with their commercial sponsors claimed that full hazardous potential would be recovered by the defective mutants passing from one host to another, (called passage), but it was not appreciated then that the bacteria would be expected to have reverted to becoming sensitive. This is precisely what we found.

This interesting theory, however, must have fooled the regulatory authorities, and I am using the kindest verb I can find.

At this stage, I'll make two further points concerning resistance to SUL and TRI. One was that amongst many of the bacteria for which these drugs were intended, up to 30% were already resistant to SUL that was viewed as near obsolete anyway. Secondly, bacteria were well known to be capable of acquiring resistance to two or more antibiotics simultaneously.

Largely, based on the mythology of these irrelevant laboratory experiments, an antibiotic dogma had emerged that patients should 'complete the course' to prevent resistance. This myth still persists. Surely, the empirical common sense approach is that the greater the antibiotic exposure, the greater the risk of encouraging the rarer resistant bacteria supplanting the sensitive. This myth has never been validated. Of course some patients do require prolonged treatment for efficacy (or cure) because of the slowness of penetration into the infection, or slowness of bacterial killing. Certainly, a patient's own immune system is also a factor.

We then studied the effect of SUL, TRI, and both together in concentrations known to occur during patient treatment. So we took body fluids such as blood and urine from healthy volunteers and added typical infecting bacteria to see what happened. Being a university department distant from patients, this was the best we could so at the time to represent the actual clinical use. In general, the poorest antibacterial effect was with SUL alone, and TRI and TRI combined with SUL were both equally better. Indeed microbiologist W. Brumfitt had previously found that TRI alone could cure urinary infections. We published our findings in journals and gave talks to doctors who were sceptical, overall. It would take more work to challenge the antibiotic mythology successfully.

A few months before, a very senior scientist in the department had been asked to make a presentation to the New York Academy of Science on SA genetics. Unfortunately, he had not done any work or been involved in such work. But he knew of my work, and approached me with the proposal that he would present my work for me and give me full credit, with my name as the first author. I agreed and wrote the paper to be published after the conference.

When the printer's proofs arrived, he was away from the department and his secretary innocently asked me to check all was well. It was not. Not only was there no acknowledgement of whose work it was, but he had altered the authors names to put his first. There was an uncanny comparison to one of the episodes of the ITV drama 'Lewis' around about 2013. At the time in the early 1970s, the advice of Lord Evans came back to me, with the added caveat about resentment towards medical doctors, by non-medical.

It was time to move on (see chapter 7).

Chapter 6
The Good Guys

This chapter refers to bacteria, not people. By the early mid-1970s, it had been established that most bacteria in most people, most of the time conferred benefit, rather than detriment to us. In normal health, parts of the body that did not have access to the outside had very few bacteria indeed. Bacteria abound and thrive in the mouth, nose and throat, upper parts of our breathing tubes, rather fewer in the gullet, stomach, and smaller intestines. The colon and rectum contain billions, perhaps a total of a hundred million million – a thousand million million. The lower parts of the female genital tract also harbour usually harmless bacteria. The skin, particularly damp skin is teaming with bacteria, many just under the surface. These good guys provide benefits to us, and we provide shelter and nutrients to them, a relationship properly described a symbiosis, although these *microbes are usually said to be 'commensals'.

I'll give three examples of benefit we obtain. The bacteria within the skin release acids from oils that are protective, the sheer numbers of bacteria in the gut compete with potentially hazardous microbes we may eat, and those in the female genital tract produce protective acid. Surely, the most successful bacteria are those that live in peace with their host, and have the opportunity to pass silently to new human hosts. Perhaps the human race should learn from bacteria, probably the first and most successful living organism and act to protect its own host, (Planet Earth)?

So how do these 'commensal' bacteria spread between us? Direct spread between the skin and readily accessible regions is easy to understand, but since there are usually no bacteria in the new born babies intestine, how do bacteria find their way in? Or put another way, how do we (people) unwittingly transfer them?

I'll leave the details for you to work out. The clue is the three F's – fingers, faeces and food!

Occasionally some bacteria enter our intestines (that is you have eaten them) that can outgrow and outlast our benign commensals. These are the causes of some types of food poisoning. Other unwanted germs (correctly referred to as parasitic) are well adapted to survive in the presence of stomach acid and can cause ulcers and other diseases.

Whilst still in the intestines, I will try and neutralise some of the media – induced confusion over one species of bacteria, namely E. *coli*. There are hundreds – quite literally – of different varieties of this germ. These are called subtypes. Everyone has – sometimes in very large numbers – E. *coli* in their intestines providing a benefit by using up any oxygen, and so allowing the large bulk of other harmless bacteria to flourish. These would otherwise be killed by oxygen and are called anaerobes.

However, sometimes E. *coli* in the gut can cause infections in the bladder and kidneys, particularly in vulnerable people. Most of our 'waterworks' are normally free of bacteria except at the end and these infections illustrate a good idea about infections namely they result from bacteria being in the wrong place.

Whilst most types of E. *coli* are harmless when in our guts, a few types producing a toxic substance that can cause inflammation in the colon and a gastro-intestinal illness. Furthermore, these types can spread between people and is entirely to be expected, by the 'three F's'.

Preventing further spread and identifying this bacterium is tricky, because it takes a few days to be certain that, for example a suspect food item or human is the source of the rare dangerous E. *coli*. We do not want all our food items to be guaranteed sterile. But we do not want our food to contain bacteria that are not part of our normal commensal's, such as *Salmonella*. I'll discuss this later, but I'll leave this section by saying that it is difficult to lay blame on individuals or food producers for what was an acceptable procedure before the occurrence of the illness.

I hope readers do accept the premise that for most of the time, these commensal bacteria and their persistence should be protected. So what might antibiotics, whether or not prescribed for actual need do to the bacteria? Most antibiotics enter the human body through ingestion, and most antibiotics are given for actual or possible infections outside the intestines. Suppose the swallowed antibiotic is not completely absorbed before it reaches the colon where most of the beneficial bacteria live? What will happen? The answers to these questions are as follows. First very few antibiotics are completely absorbed for the upper part of the gut. Secondly, even low contractions still present in the lower bowel can have a major effect on bacteria. This is seen most emphatically in animal feeds when low concentration of antibiotics did have a big effect. Thirdly, some antibiotics are more likely than others to be poorly absorbed. Fourthly, very obviously, the higher the dose, and the greater the numbers of drugs eaten, the greater the possible damaging effects. But do these effects cause human illness? The answer is, 'yes'. Women and youngsters can get an irritating (just the right word) rash due to the removal of the protective commensal bacteria, and their replacement by the yeast *Candida*, particularly by tetracycline antibiotics.

Returning to the mouth and throat, there is no doubt that certain bacteria are involved with tooth decay and gum disease. However there are large numbers of bacteria in saliva, perhaps 100,000,000 per ml. So, why are they there, and do they perform a beneficial function? Is it not also possible that their presence is of value in lessening the risk of some throat infections? I just wonder if antiseptic medication primarily aimed at tooth and gum problems might influence the risk of sore throats. I do not know these answers, but have no qualms about raising them.

Earlier, in the chapter I mentioned that few bacteria would in health be found in the body outside these regions highlighted. This does not indicate that they are never displaced into the bloodstream and can be carried further. Partly from the problems of bacteria usually from deep in the skin growing on artificial joints and so on, it is assumed now that movement away from the natural location of our commensal bacteria occurs commonly, but that our immune system , be it cells or molecules 'mop' them up. It seems that our immune system had evolved 'hand in glove' with the commensal flora. It would seem that this mopping up procedure is endangered when certain 'abnormal' substances are inserted into the body. I think the good news, ladies in particular, is that silicon was not particularly prone. But watch this space.

And of course, bacteria can gain entry to the urinary tract through the urethra (honeymoon cystitis – a wonderful piece of medical archaism) or blood, particularly if the kidney is damaged. Direct spread from the colon may also occur.

The reason for describing the role of the good guys is that I was soon to embark on research with colleagues to study the effect of different antibiotic treatments, not just on their success in curing the illness, but also the associated changes in the commensal bacteria.

To Prescribe or Not to Prescribe?

The following are simulated consultations that could well have occurred in GP surgeries and are intended to illustrate the problem of whether or not to prescribe antibiotics.

Patient 1 A woman in her late twenties has been ill for 6 days, initially with a sore throat followed by sore runny eyes, a catarrhal blocked nose, and now a cough. She works as a telephonist and is concerned that the infection she described as influenza might now spread to her children. Previously, her general health has been good, but wants antibiotics and a sick note to recuperate.

The first point the doctor will consider is that the probable cause of the infection is one of many viruses and would have been most liable to spread right at the beginning of the illness. Her children may have been its source. The patient somehow thinks that a sick note could not be justified unless she was ill enough to be 'on antibiotics'. Some patients seem to believe they are tough enough to be on these drugs. Our patient persists in the fifteen minute appointment with fears of pneumonia and the possibility of the germ spreading to her work colleagues. Time is running out for the doctor who points out that the cold may well take two weeks to run its course, and doesn't really think he has to justify the sick note with a prescription. However, that would terminate the consultation and he or she would feel that everything had been done – just in case. If the decision is made to prescribe (wrongly in my view), I wonder how many prescribers would consider the risk of antibiotic resistance?

This type of consultation is very common.

Patient 2 A mother brings her two year old boy to the 'seen urgently' section of the practice. He is hot, his skin has blotchy red marks, his eyes hate the light and he has a slight cough and is irritable. These problems developed over the last day. The doctor realises that this child has a probable severe infection that could be due to either viruses or bacteria. He or she also knows that premature treatment with antibiotics could hinder the finding of the cause of the presumed infection, and so arranges immediate admission to hospital.

Patient 3 A father brings into the surgery a six year old girl who has been 'under the weather' for about 6 weeks this winter. The main symptoms are coughs and colds. On enquiries, the father admits giving his daughter some of granddad's left over antibiotics (for a urine infection) after which she developed diarrhoea. His wife was working full time and he has part-time work. As the interview progresses, it seems that the main practical problem is the daughter's transport to school.

So the doctor arranges a blood test and chest x-ray after finding the girl's chest to sound healthy by stethoscope (these are still used!) He will try and fit the patient into an appointment in about 10 days, and might consider the social services, if the tests are unremarkable.

Patient 4 A family of four come into the surgery with the statement that they have just returned from Benidorm where the holiday was ruined by food poisoning. Exactly, how long or after which meal the illness started is not clear. However, they request antibiotics for the alleged persisting diarrhoea. Scrutiny of the previous medical notes reveals only vague employment and courageous direct questioning but the doctor reveals worrying debts. Accordingly, referral of appropriate specimens for testing is made – if they are available – and no antibiotics prescribed. Antibiotics are very rarely helpful anyway in food poisoning because either the illness results from performed protein toxins rather than whole bacteria, or from bacteria such as salmonella for which antibiotics are not helpful.

For this family, the pressure for antibiotics would be intended to support their claim for the alleged food poisoning. In practice, the doctor expected that no specimens would be forthcoming (they might well be negative) and not see the patients again for this matter.

Patient 5 A farmer for a livestock unit, aged in his fifties comes into the surgery on a planned appointment and his wife describes his problem. For about a month he has felt hot and sweaty at night, and sometimes during the day. He has not weighed himself, but his clothes do not fit as they should. He gets tired easily, but has no pain or other particular symptoms. His wife thinks he might have an infection and hopes antibiotics would be the answer.

However the doctor knows that one possible cause would be an infection acquired from animals – a so called zoonosis. These are all quite rare and can be difficult to identify. Antibiotics could make the diagnosis harder to make. So the doctor arranges a few tests including a chest x-ray, blood tests, sampling urine for 'silent' infection, whilst the patient is awaiting an outpatient appointment. In the 1960s and 1970s, the availability of many empty beds would have permitted immediate hospital admission. I think the biggest insult to the patient attending outpatients today is the parking fee (or fine!).

Patient 6 A man, aged 70 comes into the urgent surgery with his wife. He is well known to have chronic bronchitis and chronic obstructive pulmonary disease (COPD). For ten days, his cough is worse; more sputum is coming up and is of a yellowish colour. This has happened before several times in the last three years. Unfortunately, he has tried and failed to give up smoking, and our doctor is not party to a philosophy that suggests a bad social habit should deny a patient treatment.

The first check the doctor makes is to ask the patient as whether he did receive the annual flu vaccine. The answer is 'yes'! I will now digress to the flu vaccine. Influenza is a single word that describes a virus that has the capacity to constantly alter or vary. Sometimes the changes are small and academics call this an antigenic drift. Sometimes, the changes are large and this is antigenic shift. Since the first global epidemic to be studied with relatively modern facilities in 1918–1919, each new epidemic of influenza has been due mainly to the virus with new properties. Infections from the previous viruses have seemingly produced good immunity to them. This is referred to as herd immunity for strange reasons. Whilst each new major epidemic of flu can be detected with hindsight, and some seem to originate in animals, birds and in Asia, it is difficult to predict future change. This makes the creation of a vaccine to be successful against an unknown future epidemic strain nigh impossible.

If there was thought to be an impending threat from one geographical or animal source, it might be possible to make a vaccine and trial it before a global epidemic. I think air travel has put paid to this notion.

We are left in 2018 with the unsatisfactory state of affairs with the flu vaccine that it would have been effective against the strains of flu prevalent some decades ago. It is simply not possible to identify how much benefit, if any at all, this vaccine confers on future infected patients. No doubt the virologist experts who advise the Department of Health that immunity to types of flu of the past claim it is likely to protect to an extent against viruses that have not yet evolved. I am not so sure. Three other aspects of this vaccine trouble me. One is the need for an annual jab – very suggestive of a very poor vaccine. Second are the changes in the types of people who have been advised to receive it. Finally, the involvement of pharmacies that must make a profit out of it.

The potential undesirable effects from an ineffective vaccine are obvious. Injection of foreign protein might well cause problems, the cost and inconvenience of its administration, and its potential to lull recipients into a sense of false security, by giving reliance on the vaccine rather than take other action such as cutting out smoking.

However, there is also no evidence that the vaccine might not be beneficial in the prevention of future epidemics. No one knows. This uncertainty must be unique amongst human vaccines. Personally, I have been advised to receive it. I have not.

To return to our patient with the acute exacerbation of chronic bronchitis, the doctor will certainly prescribe antibiotics, hopefully for the time needed for the patient rather than 'a complete course'. The antibiotics previously prescribed would have expected to have selected out some resistant bacteria (incidentally some people seem to believe that people are resistant. No it's the bacteria). In which case, particularly if the previous antibiotics were recent, a different type of antibiotic would be a good idea, as would referral of a sample of sputum to the laboratory for testing. The treatment might need to be changed. In which case the patient might keep the unused pills!

I would.

I had joined the regional committee of consultant chemical pathologists, and like microbiology, there was a major issue of where special tests were performed. There was also some not very polite discussion about the fair allocation of funds. The smaller laboratory representatives believed that the big centres, notably Cambridge and Norwich were getting more than their fair share of basic funds. This also applied to other funds, particularly those to be spent on 'locally-organised' research. I had been on the committee that had requests by the Academic Medical Unit at Cambridge. They were rejected.

After about two years, the chairman of the group retired and I was elected chairman, and was amazed and delighted, being a part-time amateur? Perhaps the others might have thought I was the best bet to question the Professor of Biochemistry at Cambridge! However, events in my life would soon preclude this from happening.

Another committee (committees can be a very effective work avoidance ploy) I occasionally attended was the local (i.e. Norfolk) group of the British Medical Association. I'll never forget a comment actually uttered by an arrogant Norwich surgeon in response to a comment. He said, "Don't confuse me with the facts; I've already made up my mind."

Snow.

The climate in North Norfolk can be unusual. With a northerly wind, snow showers form over the land and sometimes they coalesce into heavy falls usually associated with a small area of low pressure moving south in the North Sea. These are known as polar lows. But in 1978, a strange event happened. For 48 hours, continuous light snow fell and was driven by a northeast wind. At Moorlands, we gave shelter to stranded drivers, as did the school opposite. Then I built an igloo, and the three of us managed to sit in it with a glass of sherry. Miranda was not yet three but claims she remembers it. However I am not convinced she is not remembering being told about it.

During that summer and the following years, the garden was flourishing. Stephen Calton, a microbiology scientist had erected two glasshouses up the slope in the vegetable garden. One was planted with a fairly rampant Black Hamburg grape vine. The asparagus was beginning to justify the effort needed. Carrots and some more exotic root vegetables like scorzonera grew well. Peas also tolerated the sandy conditions. But brassicas did not.

Horse manure certainly improved the flower border, and the rock garden and heather border were getting established. One day, Miranda trod on a snake; at the time we were worried, but I think it was a grass snake.

During the winter of around 1980, I had been asked to give a lecture on antibiotics in the Oxfordshire town of Banbury. I was beginning to receive quite a few invitations on these lines. Depending on the audience, the details of the talks would be evident from the previous chapter. My secretary had produced under my guidance some attempts at humorous typing errors. For example, *Staphyloccus* became *Staphylococcup* and population became copulation. I avoided trying to tell anyone what or what not to prescribe. Rather I explained 'our' system.

So I set off for Banbury early that winter's morning and the snow began falling after about half an hour. It got heavier and my grubby Ford Sierra estate ended up stuck in a snow drift in Bedfordshire. A few minutes after I had left home, because the snow had already marooned Banbury, their postgraduate centre secretary had phoned Fionna to say the lecture was cancelled, and I have to admit reluctantly that this would have been a good opportunity for a mobile phone.

I can recall only two other incidents that caused me to miss an important appointment. The first was in 1974 when from Bristol, I was considering other posts. An agent for the pharmaceutical company Sandoz (I can remember my father receiving their magazine – Triangle) had put my name forward as head of 'independent' research. I was flying to a meeting with the company in Vienna. Fog caused the plane to be diverted and after an endless train journey through Switzerland and Austria, arrived nearly a day late. I think the post could have been *bona fide* independent, but I wondered for how long? Where were any patients? I wasn't impressed by the Vienna woods, help would have been needed over property purchase; I could not see Fionna liking it; certainly not some of the music. So by mutual consent, I said no, thank you.

My last missed appointment occurred in Leeds in the mid-1980s. I was due to give the first lecture to new medical students in one of the Roger Stevens block of twenty or more lecture theatres. I had not been responsible for the details of the lecture schedules. The students did not look like medical students. The dress was overall unusual. Few wore ties. Many men had beards and quite a few arrived late. They were not as attentive as usual, but I gave my usual introduction to medical microbiology. It was not for a full fifteen minutes that someone interrupted. Yes, you have guessed. These were the wrong students, beginning their course on psychology and sociology! By the time I found 'my' students in the right lecture theatre, they had gone.

From Ashwicken, I alone, and later all three of us would visit the Crown at Gayton for meals and refreshments. I began to know some of the other punters (is this the right word?) well. There were two pairs of farmers who after being on holiday together had swapped their partners. I think two persisted in their new relationship. Two did not. A fencing expert would in 1983 come to Leeds and construct the boundary for the house I would buy.

One evening, Professor Francis O'Grady whom I recognised from meetings came in with his wife, en route from his base in Nottingham to the Norfolk coast. Francis had been co-author of the standard text book arguing strongly for certain antibiotics in combination. We exchanged a few desultory platitudes, but I am sure both secretly were wondering 'what are you doing here?'

The landlord of The Crown, Richard Turner, and his chef wife owned a bungalow at Heacham near the Norfolk coast. I would live there for some months in 1983.

One day Richard repeated a joke he had just heard on the radio.

The scene: a doctor's surgery. Patient says, "I keep getting this pain ten inches above the top of my head."

Doctor replies, "Take two of these tablets each morning thirty minutes before you wake up." I have told this to many people, who in the main can't understand the humour.

Chapter 7
Trips Abroad

From the early 1970s to the late 1990s I accepted many invitations to talk abroad. The content would be very much along the lines already mentioned and I would show slides, partly for the benefit of the audience, but also as a prop for me! I did not use notes. Neither did I use notes on giving lectures to students (I always thought my best in these was when I gave no written material at all, and the blackboard remained in its virginal state as it was at the beginning).

Some talks were sponsored by pharmaceutical companies – inevitable if drugs such as antibiotics are central to one's interest. I tried not to let the sponsor influence the gist of my talk. The occasional awkward clash of interest occurred in the U.K. when due to a policy of finding a random sponsor to a doctors' meeting, their promotional displays might clash with the content of my talk. Tricky!

Pure Science.

In 1972, I gave a brief talk to the American Society for Microbiology (ASM) in New Orleans. I had two lasting impressions. One was the enormous gulf between pure science and medicine in the U.S.A. People like me did not exist there! (Maybe they were glad.) The second was sitting literally inches away from completely naked girls prancing on the table tops in a bar.

In 1973, Ian Chopra was invited with me to Poland to contribute to a conference dedicated to *Staphylococcus aureus*. The common language was English. We had noticed a myriad of currency traders in the street shadows, and could not resist the temptation to change our pounds into the then almost valueless Zloty.

The conference began well, but then the chairman disappeared and I was asked to replace him. I did. We never did find out what had happened. After the conference, with a few days spare, and our pockets bulging with Zlotys', we took an internal flight to Krakow; very medieval and picturesque. We had previously been impressed by the rebuilt showcase of Warsaw, but troubled by the poverty of the street traders. Late one evening, on trying to find somewhere where quality food was available, we were arrested because of a curfew. Sometime later we were released and confined to our hotel awaiting our flight home. I am sure life in Poland is now much better. Or is it? Ian became a senior research convenor for a drug company, before moving to Leeds in the late 1990s.

In 1974, between leaving Bristol and moving to Kings Lynn, I spent six weeks at the request of the University of Sao Paolo in Brazil to help them develop a department for genetics. Before the visit, I had suggested some necessary chemicals and equipment. These included radioactive hydrogen and carbon. Whilst these were only mildly hazardous, careful controls were needed for their handling and measurement. On arrival at Sao Paolo, I found that these chemicals were disallowed from import.

I began by giving both formal and informal talks to students and staff, trying to make the best of the facilities there were. But unlike our fashion for lecture protocol in the U.K. when everyone endeavours to be present at the beginning and remain until the end, Brazil lectures were different. The audience drifted in and out at intervals over a nominal two hour session. I was refreshed by the strongest ground coffee that I thought was bordering on a poison.

I stayed in a single bare room in a student's hostel; in the evening visited some of the street bars with great suspicion. There were clearly dogs with rabies, bizarre and tragic sights, but rarely actually frothing at the mouth. The people were a complete range of all ethnic mixes. Adolf Hitler would have had a semantic problem here! Many seemed very young, the pollution from the badly maintained cars was unpleasant and new concrete buildings were in construction, and the sky line held a mass of cranes.

When it became clear that my input into the department would not last the full 6 weeks, with liaison through the medical facility, I went to Rio de Janeiro to talk to some of the medical staff. Before that I was shown the brilliant national collection of orchids with the study of rapid and recent evolution of that genus (I thought that their human population was also going down that path).

I remember one lecture in Rio to the children's hospital doctors. One of my slides had stuck. The operator picked up the holder at the wrong angle, and all the slides fell on the floor. He was so upset; he would not let anyone help put the thirty or so slides back in the right order. I carried on regardless. English does seem to be understood by most doctors and scientists in most countries.

I was told that most of the sand of the famous Copacabana beach had been deposited artificially, I saw someone drown there, after a traditional lunch of a potent spirit. I was shown with a deep and sincere honesty the Favelas, where the first were near the base of the hill. Within a few years the home made shanties had continued for a long way up.

The earlier ones seem to be achieving a type of semi permanency. Some had electric current and concrete walls. It was almost as if another type of evolution was unfolding. I am sure many of the unsightlier shacks had been removed before the 2016 Olympic Games. There had been a strong religious presence associated with this population explosion up the hill. I could not decide whether religion was the cause or the result of the population explosion.

This had been a very interesting trip, but was not at all like I had imagined. One reason to protect the Amazon forest is to protect plant life in the addition to animal.

Jersey

During the late 1970s and early 1980s I went to the channel island of Jersey about 60 times to contribute to brief weekend conferences for GP's. These meetings were evidently sponsored by a drugs company, but I used my standard approach about antibiotics – use when needed, use single agents, select different agents for different conditions, use minimum dose and duration that were necessary. Two events are worth recording. One is that the then youthful Dr Graham Macgregor, now the well-known low salt disciple described a recent formal dinner with some eminent heart experts. One of whom on spotting Graham, took a large pinch of salt from the table and throwing it over his shoulder onto the floor, saying, "This is what I think of your research!"

The second occurred when my talk was scheduled to extend over 11am on Remembrance Sunday. The chairman had warned me that we would have a minutes silence at that time. Just after standing a voice at the back said, "I'm remembering a certain antibacterial combination (that had been criticised)." What did he mean?

As a family, Fionna, Miranda and I also went on holiday to Jersey, once to Greve de Lecq in the north, and several times to St Brelades in the south. The amount of land committed to farm produce was small, and I am sure the name 'Jersey Royal' refers primarily to the variety that did originate from Jersey, rather than the location of potatoes grown now. One retailer claims that all of its Jersey Royals are grown in Jersey. Perhaps the trading standards would care to investigate.

The Netherlands

I made 6 trips in the late 70s and early 80s, flying mainly from Norwich airport. I felt welcome. Microbiologists in that country were also concerned about the long term effects of antibiotics on our 'good' bacteria. The understanding of English of doctors and students was such that we had many questions and discussions. My favourite part of the Netherlands was the historic province of Limburg and its capital, Maastricht. I hope today any negative associations with the European Union will be more than countered by the brilliant populism of musician Andre Rieu.

South and Central America

In 1977, Fionna came with me, initially to Venezuela. I could not decide whether I was in the first, second or third world. The density of the traffic resembled that of say Manila or Jakarta, but the cars were large American. So large that it prompted one of the sponsors to comment that the bigger the car, the smaller the brain of the driver. The lectures were I think understood fairly well, but the long ceremonial meals following were an endurance test. We didn't do any sightseeing, because I assumed there was little of note to see. Fionna must have been very bored.

In the next country, boredom was replaced by fear. On arrival at Bogata, capital of Columbia the English language newspapers had prominent coverage of a women who had had her finger cut off to thieve her ring, presumably by a member from a drug cartel. I was due to give lectures over the next few days, so would leave Fionna locked in the hotel room. I had assumed that the venues of the lectures being in different hospitals and I would give the same lecture to different audiences. This may have been partly true, but there was the same core group of personal (I use the word because I never did find who they were) who were bussed with me to each venue. No one understood English, and I was provided with an interpreter. We should have had a rehearsal. We did not. I spoke slowly and removed any semblance of humour (a word of advice to certain politicians – British humour is not necessarily appreciated abroad), and tried to vary the content. Did this just confuse the interpreter? Some of the questions that finally came back to me suggested there was a big gulf between what I had intended and what was attributed to me.

It seemed to rain incessantly which gave us a good excuse to avoid sightseeing; the message to the world. If you don't think you've been in a real foreign country, go to Columbia.

The next country reminded me of arriving in Cambridge after Felsted. After a bumpy flight on arrival in Guatemala City, the capital of the Central American republic of that name, we were greeted like Royalty. There was much evidence of an ancient civilisation. Some of the historic buildings had been reduced to tatters by earthquakes, and then left *in situ*, with no attempt at reconstruction. The earthquake damage seemed to be part of their national heritage. The language problems were much less than in Columbia, my talks seemed to be well received, and Fionna seemed happier. We were both enchanted by Lake Atitlan high up in the mountains. I cannot imagine why Guatemala is not more popular as a tourist destination.

We then went to Mexico for a few days holiday. Mexico City was dreadful, the atmosphere suffocating and at the side of the roads amongst the dead animals were recognisable dogs. At one point, our driver asked if I wanted anything. I said I wanted to go home! Not an option as we made planned visits to some of the popular coastal resorts well cleaned up for us tourists as we had become.

On reflection, it was overall a valuable experience for us, but I have doubts as to whether anyone else benefited.

I would soon be visiting another country that troubled me more than Columbia.

Portugal

A year later, I went to Portugal, and had some of the largest and enthusiastic audiences of my life. I never did find out why. In addition to the formal lecture routine, I visited the port cellars, and wondered why its popularity was in decline. At the time, Portuguese wine, a rosé apart was not really popular in the U.K., but their non-vintage wine from the mountain vineyards was memorable (I think I can remember). The old city of Coimbra was fascinating, and the black swans in the Lisbon botanical gardens had presumably made their way from Western Australia. I liked Portugal. I hope that a missing girl will not deter tourists. That event could have happened almost anywhere.

Canada

I spent in 1980 two weeks in Canada just before the first referendum by Quebec voters over possible independence for that state. This was the main topic of conversation, with those from states other than Quebec firmly opposed to independence fearing the eastern maritime states of Newfoundland and Labrador, New Brunswick and Nova Scotia would be isolated, and the whole country, including Quebec would suffer. Historically, France had had a major presence in what are now Canada and the U.S.A.

My lecture tour was hard work. Two lectures, two flights, and two sets of ceremonial events each day was the basic schedule with other diversions introduced *ad hoc*. After the eastern states I arrived in Quebec and was told confidently by the minder that the proceedings of the meeting would be in English. They were not. French was the language everyone used, apart from me. However, I could understand most of the French, with similar classical routes forming the basis of the medical terms, whether in English or French.

Toronto was next, and I had a most peculiar offer of a job. One of the consultant microbiologists at the children's hospital wanted to try his hand at speculating on the stock exchange full time and needed temporary locum for an uncertain period. Presumably, he thought I was in Canada having lost my job. I had to explain why I said, "No thank you." Curious judgement.

I learnt one lesson in Canada. Airline security staffs are a bit short on humour, certainly in Canada. Before one flight, my slides were treated with grave suspicion, particularly when asked, I denied they were gelignite. It took some time to smooth the ruffled feathers.

Something happened one night that I thought unique until cricket commentator and raconteur Henry Blofeld described his predicament on becoming locked out of his hotel room, being stark naked. It was not unique to him!

Finally to Vancouver, where my old mate, John Anderson had arrived via York. We had had much in common, particularly being the target of malice and envy by scientists without medical qualification. John had begun life with a science degree, and also like me proceeded with medical training. He was dabbling in what we call Estate Agents.

After leaving Canada, I was amused to learn that despite opinion polls suggesting a vote to independence, Quebec voted to remain part of Canada.

Libya

I gave two lectures to doctors in Libya around 1980. I was told I was the first 'foreign speaker' to be allowed into the country since Gaddafi's control. I am not sure whether or not this is something to be proud of. There were certainly many 'observers' around and my slides were checked and the observers even watched the lecture. The country seemed to me to be functioning normally, and I was shown some ancient ruins. There were no mishaps, and I did not feel in danger.

Australia

It is said that timing is everything in life, and so it was with this visit. I had been invited to Australia by the Australian Royal College of Pathologists, and the University of Western Australia with no evidence of a sponsor (meaning I went unpaid!) to be there about a month. The academic work in Perth concerned gene transfer in *Staphylococcus aureus* (SA) and was headed by Warren Grubb. The medical microbiologists in that country were not that enthusiastic about some of my conclusions. I corresponded with a recent British immigrant who had warned me over possible argument. I would not funk a challenge.

Cricket has long been a bone of contention between the Poms and those down under, and I was following the current ashes series with much foreboding. The game was being played at Headingly, Leeds. I did, of course not know that in 1983, I would be moving there.

I was making the journey on that fateful day in August 1981 to Heathrow. The taxi driver had the radio on, and it was looking like a further crushing defeat by Australia. But then Ian Botham (now Sir Ian) started batting. I continued listening and watching in Terminal 3 at Heathrow. Then almost a miracle happened. Botham scored 147 (I think) and not only would Australia have to bat again, but it was just possible that England could win the next day. There is nothing worse for a sporting side – or indeed whole nation – to have an expected victory converted to defeat. The next day, towards the end of the flight the British pilots kept us abreast of the score. Bob Willis took 8 wickets and we won.

A few weeks earlier an incident happened that had attracted a lot of attention rightly. The Pope had been stabbed, but was now recovering. Readers of this book so far will realise that my sense of humour can be slightly mischievous. So when the plane landed at Melbourne, I asked for two slides to be prepared for my first talk; 3 days later the first slides asked –

'WHAT IS THE DIFFERENCE BETWEEN THE POPE AND THE AUSTRALIAN CRICKET TEAM?'

The second slide answered –

'THE POPE IS GETTING BETTER'

The lectures went much as expected. I tried to counter the usual philosophy of the day that antibiotics use provokes more and more resistance, creating superbugs that are not only resistant, but intent on causing more harm to patients. The good guys are the microbiologists in league with the drug companies who produce an endless succession of new antibiotics.

Because of so much disagreement and vitriol, I convened my own extra meeting in Melbourne (incidentally the name comes from a small village near Cambridge). This was well attended and received. Then it was Adelaide and then Perth. There was this statement that Australia was a series of cities connected by air bridges in near the mark. I liked Perth and the university department very much and was given a tour of the alpine flowers (this was early spring) on the nearby mountains. Then I was off to Brisbane. I had spent hours walking around the zoological park and saw the famous animals. Unfortunately, by the evening, my left knee (that had become injured at school) was extremely painful and swollen, and I needed help to put on the sock and shoe the next day. But I managed to give my talk as usual and had one last piece of oral nastiness. The questioner asked whether I knew the 80:20 rule. I said no. He claimed that you can assume that 80% of the content of a talk is correct and 20% is incorrect. He went on, "How do we know which of your claims fall into the 80% category and which into the 20%?" I refused to comment on such a silly premise.

Then physiotherapy was arranged on my left knee. I did not know it was gout at the time, but the exquisite pain pulling at the joint made the diagnosis likely. This was later confirmed after my return home. Perhaps in time the Australian nation will develop more sensitivity to match their forthrightness.

Bahamas

In 1981, I was asked to chair a small conference in the old colonial Island of Grand Bahamas. The speakers would provide copies of their talks and I would be responsible for the writing of the questions and answers. All went well at the meeting. I even ventured for my only time into a Casino – and won a little! The return home was tedious with delays in Miami. In one hand I had my personal luggage and in the other the conference papers to be published as a booklet. By Heathrow, I felt exhausted, and after changing tube lines, I suddenly realised with horror that I had left the conference papers on the train! So I waited about 30 minutes, and made contact with the station at which the train would have next arrived. Amazingly, a kind person had handed the case in. My belief in the human race was restored!

General Practitioner

In the late 1980s and early 1990s, GPs were, continually required to participate in a quota of education sessions. Several ingenious groups had arranged their tuition to coincide with a holiday of their choice. For example, after speaking in Tenerife, I would fly home after talking, and their holiday would start in Ernest. Similarly, after talking at a paradise resort in Southern Thailand (I hope it survived the Tsunami of 2004), I returned to Bangkok with a meandering rail journey. The Italian resort of Viareggio was on the Ligurian Sea, off Tuscany and the return rail journey was spectacular. First, the route went through a series of tunnels along the coastal inlets and villages of Tuscany before arriving at Milan Central, more of a palace than a station. The route under and through the Swiss Alps took me to Lucerne and then Basel. I realised the French word 'express' does not indicate the fastest type of train. After a night in Paris, I was home.

Ireland

My first invitation was to Trinity College, Dublin, where the microbiology department did seem to be part of the College that could well have been mistaken for a Cambridge set up (Ireland was part of Britain up to 1922). I had been shown the famous 'Book of Kjells'. The previous microbiology work done here included the bacteria found in raw sausages that would explain their true source. Preservatives might now spoil their research.

After the meeting, I felt obliged to consume some black fluid overlaid by cream froth. This was stronger than the brand brewed in London, and while watching a cricket game on the college green, I fell asleep.

My second trip to Ireland was to Cork twenty years later as external assessor of the candidates applying for the post of Professor of Food Science. I hope the U.K. will always have a good relationship with Eire, despite our apparent attempts to create a rift in 2018.

European Trips

By the early 1970s, the British Society for Antimicrobial and Chemotherapy (BASC) was well established with a scientific journal headed by editors who would do their best to check the accuracy of its contributors from the various fields relating to such drug use. There would be many sponsored meetings in Europe and further afield. I can recall Oslo on a snowy winter's weekend, a meeting in the French Alps, and a night cruise to Sweden from Denmark on a so called floating gin palace.

This journal had published my article in 1975, pointing out that antibiotic resistance in many bacteria could be lost as well as gained. We did have, as politicians say, positive discussions (meaning arguments!).

Other Trips

Some of these were openly sponsored by at least 5 drug companies, others were official invitations from the countries' societies or governments, and I am not sure as to whether or not there was sponsorship, particularly in the Middle East. Certainly one environmentally directed meeting in Kuala Lumpur, Malaysia was supported by a Saudi millionaire. I recall an American professor casting ridicule on the current media obsession of identifying the location of genes for any type of bodily function. He was looking forward to the successful finding of the location of a gene for watching television! The Philippines and their standard medicine were more developed than I expected. There was still a major American influence there. I could not understand why the chocolate had so many insects crawling in it.

I visited South Africa in the early 1990s and was very impressed as to how the nation was evolving post-apartheid. Since then, the progress seems to have continued. Most of the doctors were English speaking in Cape Town, Port Elizabeth, Durban, Pretoria and Johannesburg. Those along the southern coast seemed more English than I was; they followed the football premier league, and most supported Manchester United. I hadn't done any football homework, but we had a common interest in cricket. I did not visit the poorer communities, but from what I saw, there seemed much optimism.

The Chinese certainly appeared very polite and interested, but I didn't think they had, in the early 1990s the confidence yet to become the number one world nation. The food did not bear much resemblance to food we class as Chinese in the U.K. I didn't ask details of its source.

My two visits to Indonesia were trouble free and the tropical paradise image was sometimes diluted by blunt Australians. English was understood well, and I could have had a long term contract as external examiner; too far. It was the Fore tribe, now within Indonesian territory that gave insight into the human disease – Creutzfeldt-Jakob (C.J.P.)

The three visits to Pakistan were in the 1990s, and there were many doctors who listened and then enjoyed the lavish food provided by the sponsors. Whilst technically alcohol free, visitors could purchase a whole bottle of spirit and consume it in a 'hidey hole' in the hotel. I didn't. I wonder what happened to the left over's? I felt completely safe then, even quite near the Afghanistan border.

I visited all the Middle East countries, except for Iran, and the depopulated Oman, and also went to Turkey and Egypt.

World Health Organisation (WHO)

In 1985, I was appointed advisor to the WHO to help proceed with their essential drugs policy. The intention was to ensure, that within resources available, the vital core of the least costly drugs were available for the whole population, usually by prescription. My remit was antibiotics, and I would receive a daily maintenance fee, and give talks to doctors and pharmacists to create an agreed 'formulary' or list for each country. I would visit Syria, Iraq, Yemen and Sudan in the mid-1980s. I came across no violence, had no intimidation and was well received. I appeared on Syrian radio, and was quoted in the newspapers. By a strange coincidence, my uncle Brian had been external examiner to the medical college in Khartoum, capital of Sudan around thirty years before. I was told he arrived by his own boat by sailing up the Nile before it bifurcated into the blue and white Nile. I doubted this.

I did have a problem with one country – Yemen, although not for my own safety. Another speaker should have accompanied me. He would have covered pain killers and anti-rheumatic treatment. He had vanished. I was asked to cover analgesics in addition to antibiotics. I have always believed that the most effective teachers know just a little more than their pupils and make a good rapport with the little extra knowledge, rather than confuse with excessive novelty. I was also a member of Leeds General Infirmary drugs committee (later to be chairman for 8 years), so I thought with homework and help from the pharmacy, I could help. So I said yes.

The first surprise was the appearance of the Yemen doctors. I was told they were Cubans who had learnt their medicine in Moscow, Russia. The first day went well with the doctors. But, in order to receive my daily allowance to pay the hotel bill, I had to queue for hours at various banks whilst a succession of staff tried to sort out the bureaucracy. This happened every day and one afternoon I was asked if I wanted to join a group of doctors 'relaxing'. I had a look. They were all chewing bunches of narcotic leaves and seemed to be in a type of trance. I did not try it.

After starting in the capital Sana'a, I was taken to the southern coastal region of Aden, a previous British Protectorate now in serious decay with abandoned rusting cars, and all manner of household litter just dumped.

Then travelling further east towards, the accommodation was a makeshift hostel and I was told I would be sharing a room with a total stranger. I said I wasn't. I don't think there was an international incident, but I stayed in a room on my own. Each of these countries needed help but for me to see the subsequent events cancel out any possible benefit from the WHO was sad indeed. I am certainly not alone in expressing dismay about American and allied policy in the Middle East over decades. I am still completely baffled as to how and why one of the leaders of an invasion of a country justified by the flawed claims of weapons of mass destruction could become 'The Peace Envoy'. This happened after Mr Blair had very publically converted to Roman Catholicism, surely a religion not followed by the great majority of the people.

Lectures at Home

The trips already described occurred over at least 20 years. I did contribute, to many courses in this country for laboratory scientists, nurses and midwives and various types of student. Up to the 1990s, I was also giving presentations to some hospital doctors. On one occasion, an angry member of parliament wanted a copy of my listed talk to York doctors. I told him, if he was that interested, he was welcome to attend! No show.

One incident of great fortune happened in 1985. After a full and demanding day's work, I was driving from Leeds via the M62, and then the M55 to the Lancashire coast to talk to a group of doctors at an unsponsored meeting. I must have momentarily dozed off. I awoke upside down with the car on its roof on a grass verge near the hard shoulder. The smell of petrol made me get out as fast as I could. The doors would not open, but the large rear door of the Sierra estate was shattered, and I escaped. Standing dazed by the car, it was with eternal thanks that a police patrol car stopped. They assessed the situation rapidly, and advised me to state that the steering went out of control rather than admit going to sleep. They did not breathalyse me, (it would have been negative) and then, gave me a lift with my slides and night case to the venue of the lecture. The police also arranged the removal of the car. It is strange how difficult it can be to thank those who really have helped you. Thank you Lancashire Police. What might have happened does not bear thinking about.

I was in time for my lecture and did not mention the accident until afterwards when I don't think they all believed me. For that and the subsequent night I did not sleep at all. I have no memory as to how I returned to Leeds or the fate of my car. It was as if my brain, like a modern computer, had been wiped clean.

Chapter 8
Yorkshire

The phone call came in August 1982. My secretary, Nicky, said it was Professor Alan Percival from Liverpool and it was private. He wanted me to apply for the post of Professor of Clinical Microbiology now vacant at Leeds. I said I had been out of university life for nearly a decade, but he ventured that I was ideal for the post. I knew Alan mainly from meetings and he was a commanding speaker. Sometimes he would show a series of pictures of Liverpool zoo animals to characterise certain non-compliant surgeons! Historically, the old department of Pathology and Bacteriology (now Microbiology) in Leeds had been the headquarters of the prestigious Journal of Pathology and Bacteriology. So I decided to visit Leeds.

Perhaps this encouraged me to believe I was then at the age of 41 to be young to remain in a final job. Miranda seemed happy at the primary school over the road. But what next? Fionna and I were agreed that Miranda would go to the best day school we could find, and Leeds provided more options than Kings Lynn.

I also wanted to continue research and the prospects for funding at Kings Lynn were beginning to look uncertain; I had already given a lecture at St. James Hospital in Leeds and had not seen the likes of the back to back terraces before. However, the post was based on the western side of Leeds in a building next door to the old Leeds General Infirmary. My informal visit in November went as expected, with good manners all round. I did clarify what the post was. My employer would be the University of Leeds and the pay would be on the medical consultant scale, and 60% of this would be provided by the NHS. In return I would be given an honorary NHS contract and be responsible for running the diagnostic laboratory and for preventing and controlling infections in most of the Leeds West Health District.

I would also be involved in training junior NHS staff and teaching medical, dental, science, some nursing and other students. This sounds an impossible role to fulfil, but with good will between university and NHS staff, this type of arrangement was common place and did succeed – at least usually. Not realising this at the time, a handful of bloody minded NHS managers could wreak havoc.

At the formal interview in February 1983 in Leeds, I was appointed Professor of Clinical Microbiology starting 1st September that year. I gave notice to the East Anglian Regional Health Authority to end my contract on August 31st 1983, and we put our house, Moorlands, in Ashwicken up for sale. It sold very rapidly. What a difference from our last move.

We needed to buy a property rapidly near Leeds, and after genuine help, an estate agent had a short list of 8 houses we viewed on Easter Monday. All were semi-rural around the North West fringes of Leeds. My father seemed interested and pleased with the move, but warned against the cold climate. Someone had said that in Yorkshire, the last day of spring was June 30th, and the first day of autumn was July 1st.

We bought Carlton Manor in East Carlton quite near the expanding Yeadon Airport. Although the house was a basic stone construction, it was a mess both inside and also outside disfigured by brown streaks from the rusting gutters. There were three and a half acres of a wooded drive and a field yet to be fenced.

We moved at the end of May 1983, having paid £86,000 for Carlton Manor. The nearness of the airport was a mixed blessing. The noise was irritating, at least initially and some friends were appalled to learn that we lived just a mile from the single runway, the end being visible from what was then 'our field'. We could also see Ilkley Moor and on a clear day the hills of Derbyshire Peak District. Inevitably, long distant views mean liability to wind damage, although not with Michael Fish's famous storm of October 1987. Over the next few years, the issue of airport noise became less, and when Carlton Manor sold in 2004, it made £895,000.

To return to more practical matters, for the next few months I returned to Kings Lynn and stayed in Richard Turners hospitable bungalow in Heacham during the week. During this time at Kings Lynn, the various groups of scientists arranged generous leaving parties, and I was beginning to question whether I had made a mistake in going. The recurring question I asked was whether I (being a Southerner and East Anglia is essentially southern in attitude) would get on with Yorkshire folk. Someone said, "A Yorkshire man is a Scotsman with all the generosity squeezed out." Why does a Yorkshire man believe the sun orbits around earth? Answer: 'Because he thinks he is the centre of the universe'. This was to be prophetic because I did feel that I wasn't accepted by some of the older consultants at Leeds General Infirmary (LGI).

I think Kings Lynn was the happiest working phase of my life and after the generous send offs, and I would later learn that I was replaced by both a Consultant Microbiologist and a Chemical Pathologist. I would also return to Kings Lynn to give an annual 'Lacey Lecture' for the next five years.

During the last few weeks at Kings Lynn, I had numerous phone calls from impatient LGI consultants asking for support in research grant applications. I gained the distinct impression of less than enthusiastic respect for my predecessor who had moved to London.

During the week ends at Carlton Manor urgent work started with our field being fenced off by a farmer I knew in Gayton. Then the iron guttering of the house was replaced by aluminium made by an extrusion process at the house. After painting over the rust streaks on the rendered outside, the house looked much better.

The inside of the house had not been upgraded to any extent since the 1930s, and many of the homemade looking cupboards were lined with copies of 1920s and 30s Yorkshire Post that did make interesting reading. The previous owners had seemingly 'camped' in just two rooms, and had now moved to the converted stables next door. Earlier owners included a Member of Parliament for Preston and the amateur captain of the Yorkshire cricket team.

Work in Leeds

Finally, now completely moved to Leeds in September 1983, a typical schedule would be as follows. I would drive from Carlton to take Miranda to Ford House, the junior school of Leeds Girls High School, then in Headingly, then call into our 'satellite' Laboratory at Chapel Allerton Hospital, act on any relevant infections, then arrive at my base, The Old Medical School, a listed brick and stone building adjacent to the LGI. There I would talk to my control of infection staff, headed by a scientist rather than the usual nurse. My secretary would present me with any urgent matters and remind me of pending commitments. I would then endeavour to sit down with trainee medical microbiologists and discuss interesting – or indeed dangerous – bacteria.

Fionna would nearly always collect Miranda from school. Meanwhile, I would plan and supervise others' research rather than being the principle operative conducting the experiments. There would be frequent meetings under the auspices of both university and the NHS and one issue that would need to be addressed urgently were the unfilled vacancies for consultant microbiologists in the Yorkshire region and both clinical and scientific lecturers at the University of Leeds.

Frequently, meetings extended over lunch times, but when I could, I joined the LGI consultant staff in their exclusive dining room. The atmosphere tended to be funereal rather than jovial as in Kings Lynn. Sometimes I felt I was sitting at the table of God!

I had noticed three other major differences between Norfolk and West Yorkshire. First, the density of the population and the traffic on the West Yorkshire roads, secondly the potholes, and thirdly the number of sandwich shops. Everyone was in an almighty rush.

It was only a few years later that I realised the cause of the near hostility of some of the senior consultants when one was escorting some other senior doctors around 'my' department. I should have twigged before that the name of the building 'The Old Medical School' meant precisely that. This was where they had trained in medicine, and after a state of the art new Medical school had been built in the 1960s, the University of Leeds had had the building converted to contain both academic and also clinical microbiology and chemical pathology for patient care.

However, our department pursued a variety of research projects with the LGI consultants. Some were administered entirely through the NHS with no problems. However, the University of Leeds seemed to be so bereft of funds for its core services that it charged a 35% administration fee on research funds. Donors of research money were not impressed, and I would have lost some grants had I not found a means to get round the problem!

In March 1984, Fionna had our second daughter, Gemma Rose who was born in the LGI Clarendon wing. All had gone well and we now had three of our seven bedrooms in Carlton Manor fully used.

During 1984, I watched with concern the events that happened at Stanley Royd Hospital, Wakefield just 12 miles to the south of Leeds. The following is a verbatim copy of what I published in 1989 (see curriculum vitae).

Stanley Royd Salmonella Outbreak

"In the U.K. our two biggest salmonella outbreaks occurred in 1984. One, at Stanley Royd Hospital, Wakefield, affected about 450 patients and staff. Nineteen vulnerable patients – long-stay elderly patients with psychiatric diseases – died. The cause – against the background of poor facilities, problems with the administration and staff morale – was a catering error: contaminated beef had been left out in the kitchen on a warm summer night. This case received a great deal of publicity. Less widely reported was the outbreak on British Airways aeroplanes the same year. There were 766 cases and two deaths. The source was apparently contaminated aspic glaze produced in a local kitchen as an accessory to a cook-chill system for the airline meals. The exact details have not been published."

During 1986, I was contacted by some consultant staff from Pinderfields Hospital to ask whether I or a colleague could provide microbiology input, because of management decisions following the salmonella outbreak. I did not have an appropriate colleague, nor could I expect a trainee to have an input. So I volunteered myself and was contracted by the Yorkshire Regional Health Authority for one session (say 4 hours) per week in addition to my other work.

At this stage, it is worth remembering that the political scene was dominated by Thatcherism policy with victories over

Argentina and the miners. The Hillsborough cover up had yet to be unearthed, and there was a philosophy amongst some sections of government that public services were wasteful and inefficient and should be replaced by initiatives from the private sector.

I was not quite aware of this, at the time, but the events at Stanley Royd would be seen by the trade unions as an extension of this philosophy into the NHS.

A new manager for the Wakefield Health Authority had already been appointed. Previously he had been a manager for a biscuit company, not to me ideal experience for NHS work. However, I am sure he was well supported by the chairman of the Yorkshire Regional Health Authority, Brian Askew, a director of another health – providing company, Samuel Smiths brewery of Tadcaster. I gather that Sir Brian later retired to Northumberland.

Whilst refrigerated meals (as opposed to frozen) were gaining popularity in the retail food trade because of speed of reheating, there was an understanding by the Department of Health and most microbiologists, that the margins of safety associated with the so-called cook-chill system were insufficient for many NHS uses.

However, a new kitchen had been constructed with little consultation as part of the following system. First, meals would be cooked in bulk outside the NHS (i.e. the private sector), then refrigerated to about +5°C, stored, and then transferred to the new kitchen, where they would be reheated in bulk, and then plated and transferred to trolleys to be trundled around the hospital over anything between half an hour and two hours, and then served to patients who, assuming they recognised the plated debris as being edible, might examine it with utensils.

It is not surprising the catering manager at Pinderfields advised me that he assumed that hospital food had no nutritional value at all.

For me, safety worries apart, this type of food production was not appropriate for patients. Meals should not only provide nutrition but should comprise an event to enlighten an otherwise dismal day.

One of the excellent scientists in the Pinderfields microbiology laboratory, Eric Lister had furnished me with an article by American scientists highlighting bacteria that could survive, and indeed multiply at temperatures just above freezing point, around +5°C – +10°C. And above that temperature these same bacteria could multiply even faster. The most dangerous of these germs was named *Listeria monocytogenes* and had been the cause of many serious episodes of infections after contaminated chilled food had been eaten. The bacterium was found widely in the environment and also in some animals, notably sheep. The foods involved included salads, coleslaw, soft crusted cheeses, cooked meats and cooked processed meats such as pâté.

Assuming that the policy of imposing cook-chill food from the private sector as proposed for Wakefield would be a general policy of the Thatcher regime, I turned as many facilities as possible into trying to assess the scale of any problem. Two of my bright trainee medical microbiologists, Kevin Kerr and Stephen Dealler were interested. Both subsequently were appointed consultants in the North of England.

Meanwhile, the arguments for and against cook-chill continued in Wakefield. Union representatives attended meetings and the local media, particularly the Yorkshire Post were well informed (incidentally, I have never been the primary source of leaks to the media, but have frequently needed to respond).

One meeting was attended by Tim Lang and his colleague Julie from The London Food Commission that had been set up by the then mayor Ken Livingstone to balance some of the propaganda of the food industry. I came to know Tim well. He was a person of impeccable integrity and became Professor of Food Policy in London. I cannot claim that cook-chill was given a warm reception by anyone. No doubt the current proposal at Wakefield was the worst possible option.

Then I was summoned to appear before the Wakefield Health Authority under the chairmanship of Sir Jack Smart of local authority repute. A union representative was in attendance, but did not have all the papers. He told me later that just before I was ushered in, each member was provided with one sheet of paper relating to me. These were then collected in before I entered. To this day, I do not know what was on that piece of paper. The most insistent inquisitor was Rodney Walker who ran a transport company based in Wakefield. He would subsequently become the famous and influential sporting guru Sir Rodney Walker.

Clearly, the minds of the members of the authority were already influenced by that sheet of paper, although I could not understand the direction of the questioning. However the media had become *au fait* with a new name for a bacterium – *Listeria*. Unfortunately, that species of journalists responsible for headlines knew the impact of rhyming slang and, inevitably, LISTERIA HYSTERIA appeared, followed, disappointingly in the 'meat' of articles, written by ethical food writer Derek Cooper for the Sunday Times. I even had one journalist from that paper pottering around my laboratory in Leeds for a whole day. I made him wear a white coat, take precautions and do something useful!

Soon, because cook-chill (renamed cook-kill by one magazine) was becoming an epidemic in its own right, the Royal College of Pathologists held a whole symposium on the issues raised. In one hospital in the Midlands where reheating was planned on each ward, not only was the financial outlay massive, but the power supply could not cope as all the reheating occurred simultaneously. A whole new electricity substation had to be constructed.

To summarise so far, the forced introduction of privatised catering into the NHS, largely through political dogma was fraught with difficulties. Defendants of the systems claimed, for example, the ready meals sold by Marks and Spencer Foods and created by Northern Foods centred in Hull were safe and of high quality. I have not criticised these products. The consumer has choice and is responsible for safety by reheating. Patients do not. I had many arguments with members of parliament who made nonsense claims about my failure to attend non-existent meetings at Northern Foods and so on. I do have however, a criticism of some of these convenience products – high prices, fixed portion sizes, and disposal of the packaging.

It was at this time that I made contact with David Hinchliffe, MP for Wakefield. David was a great fan of Rugby League, and after I visited him in Parliament, the Yorkshire Evening Post did a humorous mixed metaphor article over a misshapen rugby ball that I was attempting to correct! Humour is a very good antidote to nastiness! I also met the MP for neighbouring Halifax, Alice

Mahon. I would like to thank David now for asking many questions to the government over the next few years.

The Yorkshire Regional Health Authority under the chairman of Brian Askew from Samuel's Smith Brewery set up an inquiry with invited experts on the safety of cook-chill. I refused to contribute. It would have been comparable to attending an inquiry set up to decide whether or not a motor car was 'safe'. The experience with British Airways that employed a variant of cook-chill catering was well known with evident hazard that only 2 deaths occurred, whilst there were 19 at Stanley Royd, suggests differences in vulnerability between patients and airline passengers. Returning to the motor car, as to whether it is safe or not depends not only on how it is constructed, but on how and where it is driven. The moral with inquiries is that if a silly or inappropriate term of reference is identified, then a silly outcome can be expected.

Meanwhile, the Wakefield Authority had put in place the procedure to appoint its own consultant microbiologist and I was looking forward (yes, genuinely) to interview potential candidates. Before leaving Wakefield, I would like to pay a big tribute to many of the doctors and the other staff who were doing their damned best under difficult circumstances. I did work with the pharmacy over antibiotics, and I would talk and meet many GP's over the next few years.

Finally, the burns and plastic surgery unit impressed, particularly, and was ably and sensitively led by Dr John Settle. He would ask me to attend ward rounds in the burns unit and we would discuss the main scourge for healing burns – infections. I visited John more than once in his large house on the Leeds side of Wakefield. For a strongly patriotic Yorkshire man, he was very modest, and would soon retire to North Yorkshire to pursue his hobby of woodworking.

So it was *au revoir* to Wakefield. I think I had been confronted with the whole microcosm of our society. I felt sorry for the large post-industrial population of South and West Yorkshire, and their manipulation by a bullying regime. Stanley Royd Hospital closed in 1995.

Veterinary Products Committee

In the early 1980s, my work completed in Kings Lynn on the difficulty of transferring antibiotic resistance from strains of

Staphylococcus aureus of animal origin to those from a human source, had been published in the Scientific Journals. The conclusion was in direct contrast to the many of the views of E. S. Anderson who I had 'met' at an interview in Newcastle a decade earlier. Anderson was known affectionately (?) as Andy and was still maintaining that low or sub inhibitory concentrations of antibiotics in animal feed caused many of the resistance problems in patients. I did not.

Surely, by 1986, it was accepted that most of an animal's bacteria were well adapted to that species in question and whilst an occasional 'excursion' to a different host might cause illness, for example *Salmonella* in human beings. For any genes conferring resistance in essentially animal bacteria to become incorporated in human bacteria must be rare. Rather, I believed that most antibiotic resistance in human bacteria was due to the intensive use, and misuse of antibiotics in people.

These issues are my surmise as to why I was appointed to the Veterinary Products Committee, the group of Veterinarians, Pharmacists and Doctors 'served' by the Civil Service and was chaired by the respected and ethical Professor James Armour C. B. E. of the Glasgow Veterinary School. This committee reported to the Ministry of Agriculture.

Whilst not formally signing any 'official secrets' document, confidentiality was, rightly, expected on details of products submitted by pharmaceutical companies. I will not mention any individual product, much as I would like to, and I am sure the following will not be confidential. Our terms of reference consisted of three aspects of drugs and vaccines use in farm animals and pets. One was the quality of the product typified by its stability, purity and potency, essentially issues of pharmacy. The second was efficacy, asking whether the makers of the product had indeed provided enough evidence to show that the product did indeed have the capacity to achieve what it was intended to. And thirdly was, whether the risk of side effects, or adverse reactions, were at an acceptable incidence for the type of product. These three issues also apply to drugs used in human medicine, but for animal use, defining both efficacy and safety (lack of side effects) can be much harder than in some human use. We were also, where appropriate, asked to comment on any possible consequence of animal use to human health. I do not think that human use of pharmaceutical products is often concerned about impact on animals.

It is the omissions from our terms of reference at the time that concerned me. There was no question as to whether anyone liked, wanted, or thought they needed a product. In a fiercely competitive world, if a product caused, say increase meat yield for farmers over unit cost, then others might feel obliged to 'keep up'. Nor was cost considered. However, the biggest problems for me were the provision of information claiming a product did in practice work. We had no certain way of establishing whether or not trial information was 'lost' or cancelled if it did not support the applicant's case. It is inevitable that some trials will be abandoned prior to completion – due for example animals sold for slaughter due to commercial reasons. Ultimately, the issue was a matter of trust, and we generally did accept the totality of the information provided.

There was one particular area that troubled me then, and now in 2018. This concerns vaccinations, particularly, for dogs, because of changes – either known or suspected – in the microbe (this includes bacteria and viruses) over the years. Also, in assessing possible side effects, it must be difficult to attribute an illness in a dog to a vaccine or something else. Also, the general study of microbes in dogs is not as sophisticated as in people. I am not claiming that any vaccine in pets does or does not work, but it is difficult to be sure that efficacy in the past guarantees benefit now.

By 1987/8, plans at home were going well. Miranda was now going to the senior arm at Leeds Girls High School and Gemma beginning at Kindergarten. Both were doing well. The inside of our house was nearing completion. The kitchen had had a serious makeover with the ceiling lowered and the 1930s painted cupboards replaced by contemporary oak (I shouldn't be surprised if they had by 2018 been painted in modern distressed fashion). We had kept the 'antique' oil-fired central heating because there was no gas. We had furnished our large reception room with some more antique (genuine) guilt mirrors, had secondary double glazing installed and the large attic space was fully insulated.

Outside, the planned conversion of the field into a semi-wild woodland garden had started well. I had planted a mixture of deciduous and evergreen trees and shrubs aside a network of grassy lanes, and with the help of a local lad had begun the annual planting of unusual daffodils each August and September. We also had help from a decorator who refused to hang wall paper with images of birds – Yorkshire mythology that was news to me!

My basic work routine continued as before. After taking my daughters to their schools, I arrived at HQ in the Old medical School via Chapel Allerton.

We (our unit of clinical microbiology) had obtained a variety of new research grants and I'll highlight three. One was from the Central Electricity Generating Board (CEGB) to study the possible presence of legionella bacteria (the cause of the relatively newly identified Legionnaires disease named after those veterans who had attended a reunion in Philadelphia about 20 years earlier). This involved sampling the many large concrete funnel-shaped cooling towers of the many power stations in West Yorkshire and beyond. It was exciting and demanding work, and whilst the details remained confidential, two of our staff gained higher degrees, a doctorate and masters.

Another grant was obtained by the gastroenterology unit headed by Dr Tony Axon to take another look at the possible benefit of antibiotics in the treatment of ulcerative colitis. Previously, it was the emphatic (I think this may have been too emphatic) view that antibiotics were not helpful in this condition, that did have all the hallmarks of an acute inflammatory process typically due to an infection. With our help, in a properly planned trial Tony and his team did find that the novel antibiotic, tobramycin was of benefit. The leading medical journals refused to publish. Why? Finally, the results were published in a rather less prestigious journal.

We had several requests to do basic testing in the laboratory of new antibiotics from different American Pharmaceutical companies that had synthesized a new range of antibacterial molecules called quinolones. These did appear highly effective in killing bacteria in the laboratory but I gather side effects during their trials in patients would arrest some of their potential value.

Court Appearances

Sometimes incidents or conflicts, on which I had been asked to advise, went to court. I'll mention three anonymously. A take-away curry was found by the consumer to contain a cigarette butt. The local authority prosecuted. I defended, pointing out that whilst not aesthetically pleasing, even the consumption of a cigarette end had not been identified as a health hazard. The local authority lost. (Incidentally it could not be established as to whom was responsible for the insertion of the cigarette butt into the curry).

Secondly, another local authority prosecuted a company operating cooling towers as the source of a small outbreak of Legionnaires disease. It is very difficult to be certain that any one water source is the cause of a patient's problem. The first difficulty is that there are many different types of the legionella bacteria, and it can be difficult to know exactly which type caused the patient's illness, particularly if not all the correct samples had been sent to the laboratory. Furthermore, water sources other than that suspected have to be ruled out – meaning the patient's possible exposure in the days before his or her illness has to be considered. Whilst we did have the experience and facilities, my staff needed to do much extra work. Another problem is that samples of water can contain several different types of this bacterium. Attempting to prove a causal relationship between one source and the disease in one or a very few patients is difficult, to say the least. My lengthy report stated this and the defendants won.

Amazingly, the judge subsequently complained about my modest fee! What was he being paid?

Having thought that I would not return to Wakefield, I had a cry for help from a publican whose hostelry was located rurally between Wakefield and Doncaster. He was being prosecuted by the local authority for just using a device called an 'auto vac'. As background, and for reasons I don't understand, Yorkshire beer drinkers like the top of the fluid in the pint glass replaced by froth that is enthusiastically welcomed as a 'head'. It has always struck me a very expensive means of purchasing air! Anyway, in order to achieve this froth, the beer is pumped out through a small nozzle, and the resultant frothy fluid tends to flow over the top of the glass, and can either go to waste or be collected and returned to the beer barrel through the 'auto vac'. My report failed to find any possible perceived or actual risk from this procedure. It must be remembered that, historically, the whole objective of beer fermentation was to generate acid, with alcohol a by-product, to replace the then hazardous water. In court, I did not have a chance to say my piece as the case collapsed on the first morning in Wakefield. The prosecution, that is the environment health officers in question, had failed to establish the identity of the person pulling the beer pump. This was not the last time I would witness the combination of nastiness and stupidity. I wondered what the prosecuting team might think of their hospital food, were they admitted to Pinderfields! Anyway, the publican was acquitted and the council bore the costs. *Adieu* Wakefield.

Drugs Committee, LGI

At this time, in the late 1980s, it had been the responsibility of local health authorities to decide which drugs the pharmacy would stock and dispense, rather than rely on central dictates. I had been a member of this advisory group of consultants and pharmacists since 1983.

In 1988, I was elected chairman, and although I had not appreciated that I should have been chairman for three years, I continued for 8. Over this time, the health service management appeared delighted with the financial savings that were made. The main decisions to be made were the questions of whether or not to stock new drugs that might be expensive. As seen from the perspective of the pharmaceutical company, a new drug would be protected by patents for typically 10-15 years. This meant that during this time, other rival companies could not, without permission, market similar and cheaper (because of no research costs) drugs. When the patents expired, such protection was lost, so in order to attempt to keep its share of the market use, or indeed create better agents, the company would endeavour to make available new drugs before the patents expired. The system did encourage innovation, but frequently doctors, patients, and indeed the media were uncertain as to whether expensive new drugs were better than older ones, the safety profile of which would be known.

It was the job of this committee to attempt to make this decision. For antibiotics, my distinguished colleague Peter Hawkey gave advice. The difficult decisions often involved new drugs used in the treatment of cancer, and we would always seek advice, usually by personal attendance of the appropriate specialist. Whilst our advice for regular stocking could always be overruled by a consultant on behalf of a patient, there was a feeling of tension between the chief pharmacist and some of the senior Yorkshire consultants. Personally, I had already developed a professional thick skin of which I would need a few more layers in the future.

Teaching

For the first three years, my scientific colleague Professor Douglas Watson was head of the whole microbiology unit, but the role had now rotated to me, and I think the potential for conflict made such a unitary department impossible. Leeds University gave an image of financial crisis, and everything was driven by the need for cash from grants or fees from foreign students. I'll give two examples of problems of foreign students. First the large number of students from North Africa with relatively poor grasp of English, who were studying pure science microbiology, meant that standards did drop for all students. After graduation, the great majority of science students gave up microbiology altogether. Medical students were more committed and passed the combined pathology and microbiology after two years. Occasionally, failed students were allowed to redo the whole year. One student from the Middle East was not even allowed to follow that path, despite some 'interesting' incentives for us!

I think the science students liked the lectures by medical staff, as it showed them some of the relevance of the details of the microbes they had learnt about to real life. The university was moving towards a type of spoon-feeding whereby summaries of lectures were to be presented in advance and continuous assessment rather than exams could guarantee (?) a good degree. This was not my idea at all. I wanted to make the lectures interesting and even exciting.

All university degree courses at this time would have their standard assessed by an appropriate outside person. For example,

Max Sussman from Newcastle was one of our 'externals'. For five years, I did a similar role for Birmingham students. I liked the centre of this city, after arriving at New Street and its then imitation of a massive public toilet, the area around the concert hall impressed. An image of a large post-industrial sculpture remains with me today. The access to the University by train was unique, and I had a strange feeling of regret when I heard that Cadbury had been absorbed into Kraft Foods.

The standard of the students in Birmingham was similar to that in Leeds, and it was a pleasure to meet Professor Graham Ayliffe again, many years since our Bristol era. The students awarded the prizes, certainly deserved them. I wonder if Leeds should have awarded prizes.

Over this time, most of the research undertaken in the Old Medical School was becoming both directed and undertaken by others, and I don't think I ever failed to give credit where it was due. I realised from the events that caused my departure from Bristol (described in chapter 5) how distressing such failure can be.

One of my excellent trainees, Dr Stephen Dealler was working on the effects of microwave cooking on the destruction or otherwise of bacteria within processed food. For reasons we never understood, a myth had emerged that microwaves cook from the inside out. Not true. Quality apart, microwaves do have uses, but surely their reliance for reheating complex re-assembled meals is limited indeed.

Dangers of Success

The essential practical function of a medical microbiologist is to prevent infections in a unit, hospital, or in the community. In order to achieve this, he or she will not always be popular with everyone, particularly in the modern managed targeted clinical environment.

Sometimes after a problem has occurred, been identified and then sorted out, often very publicly in order to achieve that objective, subsequent lack of publicity might cause awareness of the reasons for the problem to disappear. Or worse, in some minds the problem never existed in the first place. Many of our national problems have been exaggerated by the deliberate use by the media of words that have ambiguous meanings or associations. Take the words: LINK, SCARE, FRESH, NATURAL, what do they actually mean? The word scare has often been used with possible dangers from food. It can mean one or two diametrically opposite observations: concern over a genuine phenomenon or false concern over an unsubstantiated or non-existent problem. It has, I believe been the use of the word 'scare' in particular that has confused people in thinking either there was a problem that is now hopefully resolved, or there was none in the first place.

Salmonella in Eggs

During the latter years of the 1980s, *Salmonella* in eggs became a national issue, and I will not here attempt to rewrite history, but rather make some oblique observations. The first is that the careful, honest and accurate work, showing the dramatic rise in *Salmonella enteritidis* from human sources was associated with eating eggs, was performed by government scientists working with confidentiality to the Department of Health. At the time this work was done then mainly in Colindale, London under the auspices of the Public Health Laboratory Service.

Independent scientists like myself were given copies of their findings as courtesy. When Edwina Currie broke the news about eggs and *Salmonella* in 1988, her consternation must surely have been with the failure of the then Ministry of Agriculture to take any action. This was essentially an inter-governmental dispute, as is so often the case. The issues must have become hopelessly confused by Edwina Curries well known relationship with John Major, soon to become Prime Minister. This liaison ended in 1988, a date that speaks volumes!

I was the messenger because I could be! Employed by the University of Leeds where freedom of opinion expression continues to be endorsed emphatically, yet having a major input into NHS and veterinary work, I had no choice, ethically other than to say what I thought was happening. Having appeared on BBC Watchdog (they failed to persuade several other scientists), I knew my skin would need to thicken up a bit more. The government's approach was pure folly. Instead of admitting there was a small but manageable problem that would be resolved without disaster, the combination of personal attacks and denials would only add fuel to the developing crisis. The analogy with football is good. Instead of playing the ball, they played the player. Unfortunately, the player can kick back.

The Prime Minister, still Margaret Thatcher went on television and proudly ate scrambled eggs. It was almost as if she thought she could frighten the *Salmonella* away, like the Argentines.

I did numerous interviews for the various media outlets. Many were obsessed with finding further ammunition against Edwina Currie. They did not get any. It seems that once the media have put their knife into a minister, they never take it out.

I wonder what John Major was thinking at the time? The Department of Health (D.O.H.) did broadcast advice over the safe cooking of eggs, adding this to the previous advice to avoid listeria, particularly for pregnant women.

Outstanding problems for the D.O.H.

Eggs 2018

Eggs are laid, packed, graded, labelled, distributed and sold at ambient temperatures. Yet the D.O.H. advises refrigeration after purchase. Why? Is not the egg 'designed' to keep safely for some weeks at high temperature for hatching? If there are bacteria present in the egg (incidentally I never had a 'bad' egg in the last 20 years), why cool them down, making cooking harder. I could see a type of logic if the egg was refrigerated throughout its life, although I can't see chickens being completely thrilled at laying their egg in a refrigerator!

Refrigerators in 2018

Why do all commercial refrigerators have obvious temperature gauges and controls? Why do domestic refrigerators, have in the main a vague control that does not predict a precise temperature anywhere. The answer may lie with the popularity of the combined deep freeze and refrigerator units. With these, I want my refrigerator central temperature to be +3°C, and I am not concerned whether my deep freeze is at -15°C or -20°C or -22°C. At the very least, why do not all the refrigerator units have a large built in temperature gauge?

Five portions of fruit and vegetables per day

The problem of issuing well-intentioned but over simplified advice is that uncertainty is raised by identifying all manner of variables including the size of a portion, and as to whether the vegetable bases of fermented drinks are included. Many vegetables consumed today had previously been stored for weeks or months in oxygen-free cold store, or were frozen, chilled in air or canned. Is not the quality of the produce more important than its quantity?

The failure of government in general to add folic acid to bread and flour products.

After all the word 'folic' comes from the Latin word 'folium' for leaf. Folic acid would seem a guaranteed safe means of protecting unborn babies in very early pregnancy before a mother is sure she is pregnant.

In 1989, I was pleased to receive an award by Ludovic Kennedy for the campaign for the Freedom of Information at the Royal Society of Arts. Also that year, after an instructional lecture on how to conduct oneself in the presence of Royalty, I was awarded the Evian health award by the late Princess Dianna at a London hotel.

Chapter 9
Conspiracy?

Our plans for Carlton Manor in the 1990s were progressing well. Inside, most of the rooms were as we wanted them. The main 30 feet reception room was furnished with a combination of contemporary soft furnishings and 18th and 19th century antique furniture and guilt wood wall mirrors. I had found that the most demanding decorating were the high ceilings despite experimenting with paint brushes tied to poles. The dining room come study had my collection of tea caddies, many dating from the 18th century. It had not registered to us then that those containing ivory segments or indeed constructed primarily in tortoise shell (actually marine turtle shell) would become increasingly 'unfashionable', because the international CITES agreement banned the sale of these items if made after 1947. Many fakes from the Far East have also had an impact on the desirability of such caddies. Ours were sold in 2004.

Upstairs, two of the bedrooms had minimal attention and were essentially storerooms. We were aware of some work that was left undone. This included attention to the rough rendering over the stone on the outside, and there was no felt under the Yorkshire stone tiles. The windows could well need replacing. Many would not open. The central heating was an expensive oil-fired system circulating through large bore pipes, but we could not really see an alternative.

The plans for the garden were coming to fruition. The derelict hard tennis court that appeared to have been in ruins since the 1960s had now been converted into a tarmac extension of our main 300 metre drive leading into a concrete garage hidden by trees. Beyond that I had developed a vegetable patch served by two wooden frame glasshouses. Along the new drive, I laid myself a patio area punctuated with cultivated squares for shrubs. Once I tripped and cut my face and hands, but still managed to make work as usual.

The one and a half acre field was now looking like a garden, and the trees and shrubs would need increasing pruning each autumn. The daffodils, most of which had been planted deeply and well by my assistant Patrick, were flourishing brilliantly, and as they were visible from Cemetery road leading to Yeadon, a few visitors had a nosey.

It was then horticultural dogma that the dead heads should be removed after flowering to encourage the bulb to replenish its vigour for next and subsequent years. But I had noticed that the daffodils planted by Leeds City Council (here I would like to congratulate them on their gardening efforts) were not dead headed, yet each year gave a magnificent display.

So you will not be surprised to read that I did an experiment with randomly allocated rows of daffodils with some to be dead headed and others not. The type used was a fairly expensive pink trumpeted variety. Over five years, there seemed to be no differences between the two arms of the experiment. The advantage of not dead heading is the provision of additional seeds that can be genetically unpredictable. Although, it might take five years for a daffodil seed to generate a flower, the wait is surely worthwhile. I have always believed that persistence is the first requirement in gardening.

Although, the grass paths between the plants were fairly narrow, there was much grass to cut and even with a ride-on mower, it would take over an hour. I had one lucky escape when the mower had somehow become entangled with a hammock suspended between two trees. I don't know how this happened, but I ended up being pinned underneath. I was rescued and amazed to be unhurt. On another occasion I hit the top of my head on a lower tree branch. Because of neck pain, a colleague arranged an x-ray, and with usual Yorkshire sympathy told me that my neck was buggered! I did several TV interviews that used my ride-on mover as an 'establishing' scene.

In the mid-1990s, we had a large conservatory erected along the south side of the house. It was designed to have a soil border along the front and sides that was about three feet high. This would later hold many cacti, all from a single packet of seeds. Once, after visiting Jerusalem, I managed to 'smuggle' two olive tree twigs from the Mount of Olives. One grew and became a semi-permanent resident in the conservatory. I grew a banana plant and many daturas (correctly Brugmansia), until an invasion by a dreadful insect pest, red spider mite. I tried all manner of chemical sprays, fumigation and biological control. All failed. However, the cacti and olive tree survived.

I am not sure what happened to the conservatory in the longer term because on selling Carlton Manor in 2004, there had been no request received or given for planning permission despite claims by the builders to have achieved just that. We should have insisted on seeing 'the permission' in writing.

With three acres of woodland and garden, wild animals thrived, in addition to our pets. Our first dog was a long-haired ginger medium sized animal of mixed parentage. Woolie was followed by Charlie purporting to be a border collie as a puppy, but his long adult legs suggested his father may have been a pointer or lurcher. Charlie would always accompany me in the garden, and wisely kept his distance from the mower. Frequently, there was a flock of sheep in the field on the other side of the fence. Charlie, trying to be a pure border collie would charge up and down our side of the fence and the whole flock would scatter. But on two occasions, I 'lost' Charlie in the garden. I finally found him in a corner whimpering and hemmed in by a single sheep. I had to rescue both animals.

Charlie would sleep at night on a cushion facing down our tree lined drive and would sometimes bark, at presumably squirrels or rabbits. A perfect guard dog, but not exactly a hypnotic!

Once a young owl fell down a chimney, and we were amazed at the silkiness of its juvenile feathers. Occasionally, deer from the Chevin Forest would arrive, but on seeing us, would exit rapidly leaping any fence or obstruction. We attempted to keep two tortoises, but they would not hibernate so they went to a tortoise sanctuary. Then we were fooled by a cunning rook. It would hop around the courtyard outside the kitchen window, apparently injured. We would feed him and he would disappear. Then one day, he was spotted striding around with two normal legs!

During the 1990s, we had two cats adored by Miranda and Gemma. Both died of kidney failure, and it was not until 2017, that I learnt of the possible reason. I knew that in human beings, one of the consequences of kidney failure is the accumulation of excess acidity in the body. The response is to attempt to correct this by eliminating the acid-generating carbon dioxide by over breathing. So is the case for cats whose apparent breathlessness can be the first obvious manifestation of kidney failure. This occurred with 'our' cats and was confirmed by the local veterinarians at Tweed House, Yeadon. What I learnt from a BBC vet programme was this; the natural diet of both small and large cats, including pets, is land animals, not fish. Poor quality fish, unsuitable for human consumption, may contain arsenic as a by-product of industrial processes that can find its way into water and fish to be eaten by cats. There seems to be a myth that fish is the natural and desirable diet for cats. It is not. My mother always fed the cats on boiled rabbit (I can still smell it!). The problem for cats is that arsenic can be deposited in the kidney and cause failure.

During the 1990s, Miranda progressed well through the senior unit of Leeds Girls High School before going to Manchester University whose Vice Chancellor was well acquainted to me without much enthusiasm. Gemma went through all three tiers of the High School after Richmond House, then to Rose Court, Ford House and the senior school prior to Loughborough University. The drive to school was becoming increasingly tedious. Leeds seemed to be expanding without serious ability to address transport access. The bus lanes helped one set of travellers at the expense of another. No wonder the High School moved later to a more accessible semi-rural site, adjacent to the boys Grammar school. I had given talks to several private and state schools in Leeds and Bradford, and I was genuinely grateful not to be asked to talk to the Girls High School. My daughters might have been very embarrassed!

One consequence of being seen on TV is the ability of almost anyone to contact you, and there were four areas that concerned members of the public, sometimes organised into pressure groups. These areas were possible atmospheric pollution from incinerators, smells and litter associated with intensive egg and poultry farms, unwanted environmental impact from slaughterhouse waste, and brown tap water. I would do what I could without charge, usually visiting the locality and writing a letter. I can recall one memorable occasion on visiting the land of Harvey Smith, the very Yorkshire show jumper because of complaints over abattoir waste being spread on his field. I was with a journalist from the Yorkshire Evening Post and we were ordered off in no uncertain way. I had been writing a brief weekly article for this newspaper at the time.

In 1990, the BSE crisis was about to intensify, and I think I managed to remain detached despite much malice, but I think my family, particularly Fionna found it harder to cope with.

Mad Cow Disease

To avoid any confusion, the above heading refers to our four legged bovine friends, and in this section I will not attempt to rewrite the phoney statistical history of the disease, but consider some unpublished ideas and events. Indeed in 1989 in Safe Shopping, Safe Cooking and Safe Eating, I was initially reassured: 'BSE is too new for us to be certain that we cannot catch it from infected cows'.

BSE stands for 'Bovine Spongiform Encephalopathy' meaning a slowly progressing infectious disease in older cattle that is fatal by causing holes in the brain. Such diseases can affect many mammals including us, but were generally uncommon and untreatable. The problem was that once such an infection had appeared in a 'new' animal it could not be predicted whether or not other species could be vulnerable.

But in the latter part of 1989, rereading this statement gave me concerns, as it did the media. My colleague Stephen Dealler had begun a careful analysis of the published work on BSE, was in contact with several researchers who were also concerned. Moreover, the governments' own figures were already beginning to exceed their own predictions and BSE was occurring in too many young cattle for the source to be simply now the contaminated feed. I felt more was needed to be done to rid us of the infected herds. And as far as the human risk was concerned, it seemed to me that instead of waiting for find out whether or not people were vulnerable, we should take action now on the basis that we were.

In May 1990, the Sunday Times led an article stating that a leading food scientist had called for the slaughter of 6 million cows, the day before I had spoken directly to the editor of the paper, Andrew Neil who now presents a BBC politics programme. The House of Commons Agriculture Committee evidently panicked and demanded that I, along with others who had expressed concern publicly, produce a document prior to attending on June 13th, 1990. With Stephen Dealler we produced a report, the key statements in the summary were:

"Many (people) may or may not be vulnerable. There is no data on which to make a prediction. The best result would be no effect at all; the worst could be the development of Creutzfeldt-Jakob on a massive scale 20-30 years hence."

In many ways, the issues involved had moral dimensions, and Stephen and I believed that our primary professional role was to prevent infections; we did feel a precautionary approach should be emphasized. I can only describe the conduct of the MPs in front of the TV cameras as being trivial and irrelevant, as if they had no understanding of the subject, other than an empirical short term desire to appear to be protecting the interest of their farming constituents. One charming MP glorified in finding one word typographically misplaced in our rushed document.

This was the second time I had been summoned before the Agriculture Committee and several aspects concern me. First, there was no input from the equivalent health organisation. Secondly, the MPs did not – and would not be expected to – understand the science. Thirdly, many scientists are not trained or capable of speaking spontaneously and coherently under the eye of TV cameras. Fourthly, as I understand it still occurs today, all parliamentary procedures are immune from the laws governing libel and slander. Why? This means an MP can be abusive as he or she wishes to a summoned witness. In the committee rooms, there is no overriding speaker or deputy as there is in the main chamber.

The chairman of the agriculture committee was, then Jerry Wiggin soon to become Sir Jerry Wiggan, an MP for the west of England. It seems that many people with whom I have argued have received knighthoods.

I think the opposition agriculture spokesperson David Clarke may have been worried privately about the conduct of his colleagues, he invited me to lunch in the House of Commons for a civilised meeting. Among things David said was that I should assume my telephone was tapped. It did occur to me that were a person to know that his phone was tapped, but that the eavesdropper assumed he did not know, then the opportunity for misinformation and chaos were almost boundless. With a colleague, one could set up almost any convincing organisation or research. Was I stepping into the fictional world of James Bond, as I would later find that Aunt Marjorie had, unwittingly? No. I continued as before. I still do not know today whether my home phone was tapped. I could not see how the hospital or university switchboards could be tapped.

The malice was not finished yet. In 1991, I had a letter from the top Inland Revenue company investigations unit in Edinburgh seeking a meeting. I was baffled and worried. We met at an accountant friend's office, and after a long list of strange questions, the tax man finally conceded, there was no problem. It took some time and ingenuity to detect the basis of the non-problem. What I learnt (and I shouldn't have) was the spying centre at Cheltenham screened international faxes, and if an authorised government agency wanted to see faxes to a named individual, then they could be recovered by placing the appropriate name into the system. Presumably this would be analogous to the current procedure for detecting mobile phone messages from possible criminals. For me, the fax related to a research grant payable to the University of Leeds from a pharmaceutical company, and was nothing to do with my income.

In 1993, I was approached by a publisher, Bob Hughes, who wanted to publish a book on BSE. Bob was South African and had previously run into conflict with the South African government pre-Mandela. He had exposed the following event. A very large consignment of maize on import was found to be contaminated with excess mycotoxins. These are potentially dangerous by-products of growing fungi and the level of mycotoxin present would indicate unacceptable process or storage in some way, and the whole consignment would be expected to be destroyed. This did not happen. Instead, enough mycotoxin-free maize was intermixed to bring the level of mycotoxin down to 'acceptable' amounts.

My book 'Mad Cow Disease – The History of BSE in Britain' was published in 1994 and it contained a careful and as far as I could tell accurate description of the events over the previous five years. Bob had set up a publishing company in Jersey; Cypsela Publications Limited, 25 Hill Street, St Helier, Jersey, JE1 1BE.

Bob told me there had been pressures on him to prevent publication. This did not happen, and several positive reviews appeared. But then Bob disappeared off the face of the world; I received no royalties, and I have no idea what happened. Should I have contacted the police?

Role of the Media

As seen from the point of view of the government, it had deflected the issue to become a dispute between a few misguided scientists and the Great British Beef Industry away from the real issue that was how and why the remains of unwanted animal carcasses and offal's became incorporated into feed of strict herbivores. I am certain that most cattle farmers had been unaware of this vile and stupid practice, but those responsible remained largely incognito, as did those responsible for use and monitoring animal feeds.

Soon the government would manage to use the European beef ban to divert these issues to a foreign policy dispute. It would not be long before a massive marketing campaign would restore – up to a point – the credibility of the cattle industry.

Other aspects of the media that concerned me included their memory span. Harold Wilson famously said a week was a long time in politics. For the news media, 24 hours would seem a marathon. Moreover, their prime self-appointed role was to embarrass government ministers or anyone else in authority. And if you appeared regularly on TV or radio, that included you (or me). Furthermore, they wanted to simply put an issue into black and white and seek its resolution within hours – certainly not 20–30 years. My essential message then, and it is still only partly resolved in 2018, was that we did not know what the impact of BSE would be in human or other animal health.

I remember doing an honest and complete interview for the BBC news that was pre-recorded. At the beginning of the broadcast, I was introduced by words to the effect that, "There are of course some scientists who believe…" My Interview, cleverly edited was followed by the introduction of the real expert who promulgated the government's view. It was not long before I had a slide made stating, "An expert is a person who pretends to agree with the government." The person concerned above has now received his rightly earned (?) knighthood! I did many of my media interviews in the old BBC media complex near the University in Leeds which reduced time and stress. Sometimes, I would sneak into The Fenton pub for a bite or that strange marooned boat, The Dry dock. I always tried to separate social life from teaching students as I felt such relationships would be awkward for both sides.

I cannot leave the issue of the media without applauding the then minister John Selwyn Gummer for his convincing scientific experiment proving the safety of beef by eating a beef burger. After all, Mrs Thatcher had done the equivalent for eggs. Politicians do not seem able to learn.

Lectures

In the 1990s, I sometimes included BSE into formal or informal talks. For example, I was due to give a talk to doctors at York District Hospital as part of their ongoing postgraduate education. It was the usual practice to talk precisely, but informally around slide illustrations. It was not usual practice to produce a full written document in advance. I was looking forward to returning to York, having been involved in their microbiology unit after their consultant Nigel Peel left. I recall one of their consultant pathologists had told me, "There was more than one way to skin a rabbit." I didn't know what exactly he meant by this, but it was probably a subtle reprimand. I would not flinch from a healthy and vigorous exchange of views (politician – speak for argument!). The MP of York came across my listed talk and appeared to have an apoplectic fit. He demanded a copy of my speech (My italics). I replied by inviting him to attend. He did not.

I gave a talk to a group of MPs in Westminster; I am not sure they really understood all the issues, or perhaps the publicity and controversy was achieving something educationally? I went to the European Parliament twice and it's strange how an attitude can change on travelling to where I still considered overseas. One Euro MP thought that BSE was the abbreviation of British Spongiform Encephalopathy! Their overriding feeling was emotional, the disgust at food herbivores having been fed offal remains of mammals. I did make it clear that the practice had been banned in July 1988. In the 1990s, the UK ministry did attempt to account for the prevalence of BSE in young animals by claiming that the ban had not been implemented fully. I was also asked if I agreed that sheep remains were the cause of BSE. Yes was the answer, but it was just possible that material from dead pets, or human waste had entered the system.

At this time most of the printer's proofs would come to my work office for checking. One came to my home, Carlton Manor. It arrived late, had been obviously opened and had a note from the post office 'found open'. Someone was trying to apply psychological pressure? Mentally, I converted the quote mentioned in chapter 7 from 'Just because you are paranoid, it does not mean that people aren't getting at you' to 'Just because people are getting at you, it does not mean you are paranoid'.

A group of North Yorkshire farmers had invited me to talk to them live. The previous meetings on TV, often with Stephen Dealler, had been set up to be confrontational with Stephen and me versus farmers or butchers, often represented by a dear old guy who claimed to have eaten beef every day for 70 years and was all systems go! (Incidentally my mother lived to be 90, despite smoking 40-60 cigarettes daily from her teens). As outlined above, I did not want to blame the farmers for the problem. Rather it was the animal feed industry and the several governments that should have been our mutual targets. I went to the venue of the meeting early to rehearse the use of the slide projector. Any thoughts of conciliation went when I learnt that the one and only dinner item was beef. I left. My absence was duly reported in next day's Yorkshire Post.

I only had one incident of intended unpleasantness at Carlton Manor from local farmers. After a heavy snowfall, a massive pile of snow had been dumped at the entrance to my long drive. I managed to drive to the road through another gate near the house, and gave a cheerful wave to the driver still in the bulldozer.

I had police protection for a week or so after my name appeared in the diary of an animal rights activist. The other name on the diary was that of a veterinarian whose car had been vandalised. I may well have referred to animal experiments performed by others, but had never had the relevant licence.

Dissuading the police that the 'protection' was unnecessary was quite a struggle.

Was the malice over? Not quite.

NHS Management

During the early 1990s, it was my turn to be chairman of the Division of Pathology, essentially a talking shop for each of the four arms of pathology at the LGI. Three of these, chemical pathology, histopathology and microbiology were combined NHS and university units. The fourth, haematology, was essentially all NHS. There had been a serious dispute in chemical pathology whereby a middle grade academic had effectively accused his professor boss of not being up to the job. By a strange coincidence, the professor had begun his career with me in Bristol, and for decades we had gone our separate ways. Many others were drawn into the rights and wrongs of the dispute that would somehow give credibility to some NHS managers' proposals.

As chairman of pathology, I would join other chair people in discussion with NHS management. On one occasion, yet a new aggressive manager lectured us, complaining that the LGI research was too fragmented and we must be coordinated into one theme. I think his post was billed as some type of NHS coordinator. To us, very much in the line of that excellent satire 'Yes Minister'. He totally failed to understand that much of NHS research was a commitment extra to routine patient care, developed patiently, slowly and thoroughly over the career of the doctor. It reflected the interests of that doctor or his group and was often carried out in association with those with similar interests in hospitals elsewhere in the U.K. or even overseas. It was a stupid and flawed concept to try streamlining research into one or a few themes on the basis of an arbitrary geographical territory.

The manager in question soon left for Singapore. Best of luck there?

Meanwhile, a new manager had been appointed to control pathology, and seemed to have the perfect career credentials – positive domineering personality and total ignorance of the nature of the subject. Soon the proposal was on the table for an 'Institute of Pathology' entirely under the auspices of the NHS.

The role of the medical school and teaching commitments were brushed aside at a stroke. It did occur to me at the time that this was a preliminary destabilizing manoeuvre appearing to be justified by the dispute in chemical pathology. I even had a visit to my office by the chief executive and chairman of the Leeds West Health Authority. The chairman was a very successful property developer. By successful, I mean financially, by converting a large area of rural land into a massive car park around some chain stores. No consultant I met had any respect for either of these. At the meeting, I explained why their proposed 'Institute of Pathology' was unworkable, and my secretary said they left with 'faces of thunder'.

In the early summer of 1994, I was relieved to escape to Pakistan from the dreadful disputes centred on the LGI. My lectures included both antibiotics and food safety to the large numbers of doctors who came. I hope I did not spoil the enjoyment of the generous buffet food.

On my return to Leeds after about 10 days, I found the following had actually happened. With me out of the country, another consultant (not from microbiology) had with management back up addressed my scientific staff of about 70 and informed them that their contracts were being transferred to another organisation – the then Public Health Laboratory Service to be based in Morley, South Leeds and far distant from the LGI. The hopeless concept of an 'Institute of Pathology' was clearly a nasty negotiating ploy.

The first action I took was to consult with the University of Leeds who had always supported me over various silly complaints from the food and farming lobbies. My job, as far as pay and conditions were concerned, was not as risk, but if I could not carry it out as appointed, I should seek independent legal advice. So I sought help from a firm of aggressive lawyers with an expert in contract law. The following was agreed. I would take early retirement at the end of March 1995 and receive a lump sum and full pension from that date. I would be re-employed as an NHS consultant with professorial status based at Chapel Allerton Hospital for three years before retiring once more. The NHS would transfer the necessary funds to the University. The total cost to the NHS would amount to about half a million pounds – lost for patient care due to a straight forward malice.

Other senior consultants were also becoming angered with the management, and must have been enthusiastic for the proposed merger with St James Hospital and other units to generate one Leeds Hospital Trust. As a consequence, the chief executive of the LGI lost his job, and retired on exactly the same day as I did. On March 31, 1995, The Yorkshire Evening Post carried a kind farewell editorial to me, and ignored the demise of the chief executive.

1995–1998

In some ways life continued as before. I would take Gemma to school in Headingly; Miranda was now at the University of Manchester. Then I would cross Leeds to my new base at Chapel Allerton where the routine work involving patient care would take less than an hour. I gradually gave up teaching and also membership of the drugs committee. I liked the cafe atmosphere of Chapel Allerton village and gave a talk in one bar.

With time on my hands, I wrote a novel that I think was too complex. The small numbers of scientific staff in our laboratory were lead effectively by Bob Jackson who maintained a strong research interest. Sometimes, we would be pestered by media phone calls and Bob obtained a device to divert 'my' phone calls. I can remember a visit from Chinese TV – a one man team of performing sound, vision interviewer and producer. I can't see this catching on in the BBC. At this time – 1995–6 – more evidence of potential or even actual harm to human health from BSE was gathering, and I continued to speak openly. When John Major was defeated by Tony Blair in 1997, I was not surprised, and I was told that the BSE issue may have been a factor.

I am afraid any enthusiasm for the new regime was completely nullified by the gratuitous invasion of Iraq.

The Ministry of Agriculture: The Ministry of Truth.

This was the title I submitted for the annual George Orwell memorial lecture in 1996. I had been kindly invited by the author's son, Richard, and when the open lecture was trailed in the Guardian newspaper, I wondered whether the then leader of the opposition, Tony Blair might change his name since George Orwell's actual name was Eric Blair. Most people are familiar with the gist of Orwell's famous iconobook, Nineteen eighty-four published in 1949, so I will remind readers of the first and last sentences, respectively, 'It was a bright cold day in April, and the clocks were striking thirteen' and 'He loved Big Brother'. Whilst Orwell had socialistic sympathies, the name of the central character, Winston Smith, reminds me of something my mother had mentioned years ago. That was the reason why labour won the 1945 general election was that many voters believed that Winston Churchill would remain in control. Might Orwell have described Churchill as the best Labour prime minister we never had, and Tony Blair as the worst Conservative. Perhaps, if Tony Blair were to visit certain regions of the Middle East now, he might well want to change his name!

By 1996, six years had elapsed since my suggestion that 6 million cattle needed to be culled to eliminate BSE. However, only a small proportion of this had occurred, mainly because of the near impossibility of identifying animals that were infected, but not yet obviously ill. Two opposing pressures were at this time influencing the Ministry of Agriculture. One was the need to demonstrate to the world that BSE was on the rapid decline as predicted. This meant the provision of the smallest number of actual cases as was plausible. This would be associated with minimal financial compensation. The other pressure was the conflicting need to support financially the threatened cattle industry. By 1996, there was very near uniform agreement that BSE resulted initially from the animal feed industry, and farmers 'on the ground' were innocent parties. The ban on feeding ruminants with material containing animal protein was instituted in July 1988. Cattle numbers diagnosed with BSE during 1992 and 1993 should have fallen rapidly. This did not happen, and many BSE animals had been born after July, 1988. Despite this, the Ministry continued to claim that cattle were a 'dead-end host', and that BSE could not spread between animals. Put another way, BSE was unique amongst this group of diseases known as TRANSMISSIBLE SPONGIFORM ENCEPHALOPATHIES, being a non-infectious infection! George Orwell died in January 1950, soon after the publication of 1984 and had suffered from a very serious acquired human infection. He might well have described this ministerial *doublethink* as MAFFSPEAK. Or to update it – DEFRATALK.

By late 1994, more than 12,000 BSE cattle had been identified that had been born after the feed ban of 1988, and this, together with the evidence indicated to me (see book Mad Cow Disease in curriculum vitae) that BSE was now endemic. Would Orwell class me as a 'thought criminal' for venturing such an idea?

The lecture proceeded without incident which was a pleasant surprise, and Richard Blair hosted a delightful evening dinner event. Usually, I find such an occasion somewhat tiresome. Not this time. Perhaps we all admired George Orwell's determination to pursue various causes so vigorously.

Footnote

A serious outbreak of Foot and Mouth Disease (FMD) occurred in the U.K. during the spring and summer of 2001. This virus infection can spread easily amongst many farm animals, notably pigs, sheep and cattle, but almost never produces a serious illness in human beings. Historically, a previous outbreak occurred in Shropshire in 1967, and the European Union has been effectively clear of FMD for decades. The U.K. 2001 outbreak was caused by an Asian strain of FMD that was thought by the authorities to have been introduced through defective pig feed. A combination of isolation policies and slaughtering resulted in the destruction of about 10 million cattle and sheep. Apparently, the outbreak delayed the general election in 2001 for a month, and there was a major negative impact on sporting leisure activities. However, by October 2001 the disease was deemed to be extinguished.

The key question about this outbreak was how such a massive problem – both numerically and territorially – could have developed so rapidly, even for a highly contagious animal infection. Journalists were suspicious of the possible involvement of human activity, and it was put to me that the infection spread could have been deliberate. I discounted this very cynical concept, and I took comfort in the knowledge that human beings were not at serious risk, and refused to become involved in the debate. No doubt many cattle incubating BSE would have been destroyed during this cull.

Vaccines Against FMD

The virus that causes FMD has been observed to evolve through many large and small genetic changes over recent decades. This is precisely analogous to such variation in the influenza virus (see chapter 6).

Many vaccines have been developed against the different types of FMD virus. In several countries, laboratory stocks of these viruses are kept securely for two main reasons – as 'standards' for diagnostic purposes in suspect infections, and also to develop, hopefully, effective vaccines. There is now abundant evidence that whist a vaccine may have success against one particular FMD virus type, it may confer little or usually no protection against infections due to other types.

One such laboratory is the American/French unit at Pirbright, Surrey. During 2007, two outbreaks of FMD occurred in Surrey farms, some miles distant from the laboratory, and according to Wikipedia in 2018, the types of FMD causing the farm diseases were similar to an experimental vaccine type held by that laboratory. The most infamous example of a virus 'escaping' from its laboratory containment was that of the smallpox. This episode resulted in the destruction of most of the existing depositions of this virus, world-wide, the clinical disease being extinct.

For FMD, the difficulty of developing a satisfactory single vaccine against many types and subtypes has influenced many countries in abandoning the reliance on vaccination. This accounts for the preferred means of control by quarantine and slaughter as occurred in the 2001 U.K. outbreak. The problems for the deployment of vaccines against human influenza are very similar to that of FMD, except that the alternative means of FMD control are not appropriate! Each year our authorities in the U.K. exhort many of us to receive the influenza vaccine without any certain knowledge of benefit.

During the winter season, the high atmospheric humidity and low levels of ultraviolet irradiation from the sun encourage the transmission of many respiratory infections between people in close proximity. But during the winter, other types of illness may well peak in their annual incidence and late winter typically witnesses the highest mortality rate. This does mean that more patients do present for treatment in winter, and that when the

NHS facilities progressively become less and less adequate, it is to be expected that the first real crisis will occur in the winter.

I feel that the issue of influenza and the doubtful benefit of vaccination have diverted our attention from the fundamental shortage of staff and all the other facilities in the NHS as a whole.

Coda

In this annotation, based on several decades of experience of both universities and the NHS, I shall make some suggestions about which there may not be universal concurrence.

Universities

In the decade between leaving Bristol in the 1970s and arriving in Leeds, the most obvious change was the new 1preoccupation in the search for external funding. This was partly met by teaching foreign students and the diversion of money from research grants. Both had adverse consequences in that the language problems generated in teaching could reduce the standards for all, and also the reliance on funding from large commercial sources could inhibit the freedom of expression held so preciously by universities then, and, gratefully reclaimed recently.

The student fees and loan arrangements must have helped matters as seen from the point of view of the universities, providing the other income was protected.

However, a troubling anomaly has developed in that Scottish residents pay neither tuition fees for respective places in Scottish universities or for NHS prescriptions. This does in effect discriminate against students and the public as a whole within the rest of the U.K. Once regional parliaments had been founded and given subsequent powers, this discrepancy became inevitable. Put another way, the rest of the U.K. appears to be subsidising Scotland. This is not fair. Since so-called government money is derived from taxation, many people will want to know details of taxation income expressed per head of each country's population. They may also want to know the full disclosure of money transferred to Edinburgh, Belfast and Cardiff from Westminster. There are some vague and agreed (by whom?) formulae concerning this, but a full and open analysis should be interesting. So interesting in fact, that I am sure very large obstacles will be presented in order to prevent this. Surely one other consequence of these anomalies is the need for an English Parliament.

My daughter has recently moved to Edinburgh with her husband and my three grandchildren. I am sure she need not fear the re-introduction of tuition fees, as I have every confidence in the anticipated failure of the Westminster politicians to address this. After all, we do live in a 'pseudodemocracy'!

NHS

In the 1960s, there was some evident spare bed capacity; this was taken up during the 1970s and the 1980s that I believe were the best years of the NHS for providing treatment and compassion (when was that word last used in the NHS?). Since those optimistic decades, demands have outstripped resources, bringing us to our present endemic crisis. I believe that the following factors are at play, and our politicians do not understand, or do not want to understand these issues.

Population

Up to the last year (2017), the annual net migration to the U.K. was running at around 300,000. The birth rate continues without little effort for it to be modified. Inevitably, our national infrastructure is adversely affected. Our economic theory is seemingly determined by that sacred cow (I have been itching to use that phrase for a long time) that is called 'growth'. Inevitably, this also involves people, and the rising population would appear to be part of our national policy – if there was such a thing. Two very load voices have contributed to the debate on economics and population growth. These are Prince Charles and Sir David Attenborough. For me, the message is clear; the U.K. is full. The world is also full (charities please note). The issue is not exclusively related to climate change, but extends to the destruction of the habitat of many living species. How often has a politician become involved in this debate?

Medical Advances

Partly because of the enthusiasm and efforts of medical and many other NHS staff, and also advances learnt overseas, and also by sections of the pharmaceutical industry, innovations in medical care have been translated into real practical benefit to patients. I believe the most decisive improvements have come in anaesthesia whereby surgical patients can now be treated far more quickly than before. The advances also allow patients to be treated safely at an older age than previously. Were there to be a limited or finite number of patients requiring treatment, then beds could have been closed without problems. But the demand for treatment seems almost endless. For example, when the late Queen Mother had her well-publicised hip surgery at the age of 99, the potential demand was clear to see.

Certainly, improvements in NHS care have increased our life expectancy, and most of us are very grateful. However, I do not think it is fully appreciated that the older a person becomes, he or she is more liable to suffer other ailments, each necessarily contributing more pressure on the NHS.

Welfare State

After four generations of the expectation of essentially free education up to university, free maternity services with all the fringe benefits, free NHS care in general and all manner of benefits and pension guarantees, the Welfare State culture now seems almost part of our DNA. I am not critical of any of these provisions specifically, but the expectation of these to be always available is there. For the NHS, we all believe, I think, we have a human right to attend a GP or local casualty. It is inevitable that these are where the crises develop – at least initially.

Is there a solution?

The notion that charging patients for particular services, for example those drunk in casualty is fraught with difficulty, perhaps deterring people who may have a glass of wine who should have sought help. I have always been opposed to the prescription charge. First, it is a levy comparable to the poll tax or BBC licence fee (that needs amending), and secondly, some people are financially unable to process their prescriptions. Thirdly, the charge may well be much greater than the cost of the drugs, making it an NHS tax. Fourthly, the charge has encouraged the formulation of medicines that contain mixtures of drugs that may not necessarily be in the ideal proportion for any one person.

Of the charges levied on patients, the most irritating must be that of car parking. It is not just the issue of money, but often the hassle needed to organise one's entrance, and also exit. This charge must stop.

The response of the politicians to the growing NHS crisis has been dreadful, and always seems to exploit their own party political dogma. One party claims that more patients have been treated than ever before. The other party claims that more and more money is needed. For those with certain knowledge that additional funds have been provided to the NHS, the use of the term 'cut' must be irritating indeed. Both the two essential claims – more patients have been treated and more money is needed – are, of course true, but do not address the problem 'in the long term'. I have highlighted this phrase, because this is whereby the problem has not been resolved. A few years ago a journalist describing the raucous and bellicose exchange in parliament with an unfortunate (?) slip of the tongue reported the lower chamber as the 'house of clowns'. I do not think many MPs understand the psyche of NHS staff in that those working for the NHS really want to achieve as much as they can for others. They are not intent on exploiting difficulties in the NHS to publicise party political dogma.

During medical training and practice, doctors and other staff do learn the best means of deploying finite resources and do not need randomly calculated targets often imposed by tiers of management ignorant of the true complexity of the issues. It is no wonder that morale amongst NHS staff is now desperate, with many GPs seeking early retirement. One solution might be to ask the Monarch to be responsible for the NHS. I do not think this would be fair or practical. I await one possible event with interest, namely were the Monarch to insist on modifying, or indeed not signing at all a piece of legislation that he or she through reasons of conscious could not accept. I think I know where the public sentiment would be. Because I believe that we do not live in a true democracy, the proposal I shall now make provides a move in the right direction.

Two aspects of Tony Blair's Iraq invasion troubled me. One was the initial justification on the claim of the certain existence of weapons of mass destruction. When these were not found, the reason for the invasion became the replacement of a dictator by a democracy, implying we were proceeding from the morality of our true democracy. The House of Commons is elected, but The Lords is not and can ultimately be overruled by the commons through the Parliament Act. This means that a handful of large political parties in one house have all the ultimate power. My proposal is to elect an English Parliament to address the crucial NHS issues: these are as to whether significant extra money from taxation should be transferred to it, or, if not, how the NHS user should contribute, or whether a type of insurance should be developed. There seems little scope for further efficiency savings, except perhaps in some of the tiers of management.

For an elected English Parliament, I believe its constitution should prevent any political party from sponsoring more than a certain percentage of the contested seats. Somehow, the NHS must escape from the party political prejudice. Surely, many people consider the NHS is too valuable for it to continue to be subjected to the many futile exchanges in the lower house. I can see no reason why, for example, religious groups, business interests, environmentalists, trade unions, and even NHS staff could not sponsor electoral candidates.

Meanwhile, we must hope that our NHS staff will continue to do their utmost for others, despite the failures of our political system.

Academic Curriculum Vitae – Summary

Richard Westgarth Lacey, born 11/10/1940, Erith, Kent, U.K., elder son of Jack Westgarth Lacey, former GP and consultant pathologist, grandson of founder of The Cambridge News, and son of Sybil Lacey. Evacuated to Peebles up to 1945, followed by primary schools in London and Chelmsford, followed by Gadebridge Park, Hertfordshire and Felsted School, Essex.

Attended Jesus College, Cambridge, 1958–1961, and the London Hospital 1961–1964.

Qualifications B.A., M.A., M.B., B. chir., M.D., Cambridge, 1961–1968.

D. C. H. (Diploma in Child Health 1966)

Ph. D. University of Bristol, 1974

F. R. C. Path. (Fellow of the Royal college of Pathologists) 1968

Prizes and awards Letheby Prize in Chemical Pathology, The London Hospital 1964

Arnold Thompson Prize in Diseases of Children, The London Hospital Medical College, 1964.

Hutchinson Prize, The London Hospital, 1970.

Arnold Skerret Prize, University of Bristol, 1973.

Award from the Campaign for the Freedom of Information, 1989.

Evian Health prize, 1989.

Employment

Junior hospital doctor, London, Eastbourne, Bristol 1964–1968.

Lecturer, then, Reader in Clinical Microbiology, University of Bristol, 1968–1974.

Consultant in infectious diseases at Kings Lynn, East Anglia 1974–1983.

Consultant in Chemical Pathology, at Kings Lynn, 1976–1983.

Visiting Professor, University of Sao Paolo, Brazil, 1974.

Professor of Clinical Microbiology, Leeds 1983–1995.

Consultant to World Health Organisation, from 1985.

Consultant to Wakefield Health Authority, 1985–1986.

Member of the Veterinary Products Committee for the Ministry of Agriculture, 1986–1990.

Consultant in Microbiology, Leeds Hospitals, 1995–1998.

Retired in 1998 with status of Emeritus Professor, University of Leeds.

Published Work

About 200 scientific papers, many co-authored, in journals including The Lancet, British Medical Journal, Annals of the New York Academy of Sciences, Journals of General and Medical Microbiology, British Food Journal, Journal of Clinical Pathology.

Books:

(a) Factual

Safe Shopping, Safe Cooking, Safe Eating, Penguin 1989.

Unfit for Human Consumption, Souvenir Press, 1991.

Hard to swallow; a brief history of food. Cambridge University Press, 1994.

Mad Cow Disease, Cypsela, 1994.

Poison on a Plate, Metro, 1998.

(b) Fiction

1. Red, Yellow and Blue make White, Carlton Manor Publishing, 1997.

Postscript

Attributed to French pre-impressionist painter Edouard Manet on receipt of the Legion of Honour – "If there is anyone in this room whom I have not insulted, I must apologise."

Lightning Source UK Ltd.
Milton Keynes UK
UKHW022131260819
348644UK00018B/438/P